THE
SHAD

OW® NOW

WRITTEN BY **DAVID LISS**

ART BY **COLTON WORLEY**

LETTERS BY **ROB STEEN**

AND **SIMON BOWLAND**

COLLECTION COVER BY **TIM BRADSTREET**

SPECIAL THANKS TO **JERRY BIRENZ, ANTHONY TOLLIN,**

AND **MICHAEL USLAN**

THE SHADOW CREATED BY **WALTER B. GIBSON**

Visit us online at **www.DYNAMITE.com**
Follow us on Twitter **@dynamitecomics**
Like us on Facebook **/Dynamitecomics**
Watch us on YouTube **/Dynamitecomics**

First Printing
ISBN-10: 1-60690-562-7
ISBN-13: 978-1-60690-562-3
10 9 8 7 6 5 4 3 2 1

ISSUE #1 COVER
ART BY **TIM BRADSTREET**

ISSUE #1 COVER
ART BY **COLTON WORLEY**

YOU LEAVE TOWN FOR A FEW DECADES....
...AND EVERYTHING GOES TO HELL.
THE WORLD HAS ALWAYS NEEDED MEN WHO ACT OUTSIDE THE LAW. MEN WILLING TO LIVE IN THE SHADOWS.
BUT YOU CAN'T STAY IN THE SHADOWS ALL THE TIME.
BOOM
AS LAMONT CRANSTON III, I HIDE IN PLAIN SIGHT, PRETENDING TO BE MY OWN GRANDSON. THE ANTI-AGING TECHNIQUES I LEARNED IN THE EAST CREATE A FEW OBSTACLES, BUT THEY'RE NOT HARD TO GET AROUND.
HE LOOKS EXACTLY LIKE HIS GRANDFATHER.
NO, I'M TELLING YOU. IT'S HIS FATHER. LOOKS JUST LIKE HIM.
GIBSON
ANOTHER EXPLOSION. THIS ONE'S A BANK ROBBERY. I CAN'T BELIEVE NO ONE IS PUTTING A STOP TO THIS.
SO, I TOLD HER, THAT'S, LIKE, SO UNCOOL--
I'M VERY SORRY, BUT I'VE GOT TO GO.
WE'RE IN THE MIDDLE OF LUNCH. THAT'S, LIKE, SO UNCOOL.
IT'S BEEN GOING ON FOR WEEKS NOW.
ALL OVER NEW YORK - BOMBS, RPG ATTACKS, GRENADES. ASSAULTS AGAINST BANKS, BUSINESSES, PRIVATE HOMES OF THE WEALTHY. THE PUNDITS CALL IT TERRORISM, BUT THERE'S NO POLITICAL AGENDA HERE.
I CALL IT SOMETHING ELSE.

THAT NIGHT.
BROOKLYN.
I CALL IT *CRIME*.
AND THAT MAKES IT *MY* BUSINESS.
THE COPS DO THINGS BY THE *BOOK* - LIKE THEY *SHOULD*. THAT'S THEIR JOB.
I TAKE A MORE *DIRECT* ROUTE. THAT'S MY JOB.
THAT'S WHY THEY'RE STILL LOOKING FOR THE TRAIL, AND I'VE TRACED THE CRIMES TO THEIR *SOURCE*.
RUSSIAN MAFIA. THEY'VE BECOME MAJOR PLAYERS IN MY ABSENCE, AND NOW THEY'VE GROWN TOO FEARLESS. TONIGHT THEY'RE FINISHED.
WORD ON THE STREET IS THAT THE BOSS, ANDRE "BLACK BEAR" PERMYAKOV, IS BEHIND THE ATTACKS. HE RUNS HIS OPERATION OUT OF AN OLD APARTMENT BUILDING IN CONEY ISLAND
YOU HEAR NOISE? SOUNDS LIKE SOME CRAZY PERSON LAUGHTER, NO?
THIS IS NOT SOMETHING USUAL,

BLAM
BLAM
BLAM
BLAM

MEDITATION AND REJUVENATION IN THE HIDDEN ENCLAVE OF SHAMBHALA HAS ITS ADVANTAGES.
HA HA HA HA HA HA!!! DID YOU THINK YOU WOULD NOT BE CAUGHT? DID YOU THINK I WOULDN'T KNOW?
HE IS DEVIL. RUN!
BUT I'VE MISSED THIS.
THE SHADOW KNOWS.
WHERE IS YOUR BOSS?
THESE THUGS THINK THEY'RE INVULNERABLE. THEY ALWAYS CAVE. THEIR FEAR ALWAYS BRINGS THEM DOWN.
BACK THEN. TODAY. MAKES NO DIFFERENCE. DIFFERENT HAIRCUTS, BUT THE SAME SCUM.

END OF THE LINE, PERMYAKOV.
0:03
OH, HELL.
BOOM

WESTCHESTER COUNTY.
THE NEXT MORNING.
THE CRANSTON ESTATE.
THANK YOU, STEVENS.
YES, SIR.
I WAS SET UP. I WAS PLAYED. I DON'T MUCH CARE FOR THAT.
AND WHOEVER IS BEHIND THESE CRIMES SHOWS NO SIGN OF STOPPING.
TWO MORE ATTACKS LAST NIGHT. I READ A JEWELRY STORE GOT HIT WITH WITH AN RPG.
SOMEONE OUGHT TO DO SOMETHING, DON'T YOU THINK?
ALLARD MARINE INSURANCE

WHILE I WAS GONE, I MADE ARRANGEMENTS FOR MY WORK TO BE DONE BY A NETWORK OF AGENTS. THEY'VE BEEN KEEPING THE CITY'S SCUM IN LINE FOR ME.
ONLY THE TWO MOST SENIOR PEOPLE ARE SUPPOSED TO KNOW THAT I'M THE SHADOW. AS FAR AS EVERYONE ELSE IS CONCERNED, I'M JUST A WEALTHY PATRON.
GOOD MORNING, MR. CRANSTON.
GOOD MORNING, AMELIA.
Mavis Lockhart. Director of the Shadow Network.
MAVIS IS THE DAUGHTER OF ONE OF MY ORIGINAL AGENTS. WHILE I'VE BEEN GONE, SHE'S THE ONE WHO'S KEPT THE NETWORK TOGETHER. NOW THAT I'M BACK, SHE KEEPS IT RUNNING SO I CAN FOCUS ON THE IMPORTANT THINGS.
I NEED THE POLICE REPORT FROM LAST NIGHT'S INCIDENT, AND I NEED IT AN HOUR AGO.
YES, MA'AM.
MARGO FORYSTHE. GRANDDAUGHTER OF MARGO LANE, MY GIRLFRIEND YEARS AGO. POTENTIALLY AWKWARD, BUT WE HAVEN'T HAD MUCH CONTACT. YET.
LET'S TALK, MAVIS.
KYLE VINCENT IS THE GRANDSON OF ONE OF MY ORIGINAL AGENTS. HE'S SECOND IN COMMAND.
THE INTEL WAS BAD. SOMEONE SET ME UP. SOMEONE KNEW I WAS COMING AND TRIED TO KILL ME.
YOU WERE OPERATING ON YOUR INTEL.
IDEALLY WE SHOULD HAVE REALIZED THE INTEL WAS BAD. THAT WAS OUR MISTAKE, MR. CRANSTON, AND WE TAKE FULL RESPONSIBILITY.
THIS ISN'T ABOUT ASSIGNING BLAME, KYLE. IT'S ABOUT RESULTS.
YEAH, WELL, WE'VE BEEN COMING UP SHORT IN THAT DEPARTMENT LATELY, HAVEN'T WE?
THIS NETWORK IS DOING EVERYTHING HUMANLY POSSIBLE TO TRACE THESE CRIMES TO THEIR SOURCE.

"EVERYONE IS WORKING AROUND THE CLOCK ON THIS.
"OUR AGENTS HAVE INFILTRATED THE INVESTIGATION ON ALL LEVELS."
AND THE MAN YOU SAW RUNNING INTO THE BUILDING - WHAT DID HE LOOK LIKE?
HE WORE A MASK. I COULDN'T TELL.
I'M SORRY TO BOTHER YOU, CAPTAIN. I KNOW THAT YOU'RE SO BUSY, BUT I'M JUST SO SCARED.
KEEP HIM BUSY....ONE MORE MINUTE....
THESE FBI FILES SHOULD REVEAL A FEW THINGS, IF WE'RE LUCKY.
MAVIS, NO ONE IS SAYING YOU'RE SCREWING UP, BUT YOU'VE BEEN DOING THIS A LONG TIME. ALL I'M SAYING IS MAYBE YOU NEED A BREAK. YOU'RE NOT AS YOUNG AS YOU USED TO BE.
I APPRECIATE YOUR CONCERN FOR MY WELL-BEING, KYLE. HOWEVER, IN MY VIEW, YOUTH IS NO SUBSTITUTE FOR EXPERIENCE.
WHAT IS IT MARGO?
THERE'S BEEN ANOTHER ATTACK. IT'S THE METROPOLITAN MUSEUM OF ART.

EXCLUSIVE
LIVE
MASSIVE EXPLOSION AT MET
CNN
...AT LEAST SEVEN KILLED AND TWENTY INJURED IN THE LATEST ATTACK. THERE'S STILL NO WORD ON HOW MANY PIECES OF ART WERE TAKEN--
WE'RE DONE TALKING. IT'S TIME TO ACT.
EXCLUSIVE
LIVE
MASSIVE EXPLOSION AT MET
CNN
MR. CRANSTON, I HOPE I'M NOT OUT OF LINE, AND I DON'T MEAN TO BE DISRESPECTFUL TO MS. LOCKHART. SHE'S DONE AN *AMAZING* JOB FOR A LONG TIME. BUT I THINK SHE'S LETTING THINGS *SLIP* THROUGH HER FINGERS.
I JUST THINK IT WOULD BE BETTER FOR HER - BETTER FOR EVERYONE - IF SHE WERE ALLOWED TO LEAVE AS THE *HERO* SHE IS.
I DON'T WANT HER TO HAVE TO GO BECAUSE SHE MESSED UP. I DON'T WANT HER TO HAVE TO LIVE IN RETIREMENT KNOWING PEOPLE DIED, BECAUSE SHE MADE *MISTAKES*.
WE'LL TALK MORE WHEN I GET BACK.

RESEARCH, INTELLIGENCE, INVESTIGATION. THEY'RE ALL IMPORTANT. BUT SOMETIMES STRATEGY ISN'T ENOUGH. SOMETIMES YOU HAVE TO TURN OVER A WHOLE LOT OF ROCKS AND SEE WHAT KIND OF BUGS ARE CRAWLING UNDERNEATH.
THEY JUST GAVE ME THE MONEY AND SAID IF THE SHADOW ASKED, TO POINT THEM TO THE RUSSIANS. I ONLY DID IT FOR THE MONEY.
GIVE ME A NAME.
"A LAWYER. ANDREW ANDERSON."
MR. ANDERSON, WHY HAVE YOU BEEN FEEDING ME MISINFORMATION.
A CLIENT WANTED ME TO ARRANGE IT. I SHOULDN'T HAVE DONE IT, BUT THE MONEY WAS TOO GOOD.
THE LAWYER SENT ME TO THIS CLOWN, NAMED FRANKLIN. FIVE ARRESTS FOR DWI, FIVE ACQUITTALS. CRAPPY APARTMENT, SO HOW'S HE AFFORDING TO PAY A LAWYER TO FEED INFORMATION ON THE STREETS?
I WASN'T SUPPOSED TO, BUT I HEARD A NAME. I THINK IF THEY KNEW I'D HEARD IT THEY WOULD HAVE KILLED ME.
TELL ME THE NAME OR I WILL KILL YOU.
KHAN. SHIWAN KHAN. DOES THAT MEAN ANYTHING?

METROPOLITAN CORRECTIONAL CENTER. DOWNTOWN MANHATTAN.
ONE OF THE LAST THINGS I DID BEFORE I RETURNED TO THE EAST WAS TO MAKE SURE SHIWAN KHAN ENDED UP BEHIND BARS.
YEARS BEFORE.
SHIWAN KHAN WAS THE MOST DANGEROUS ENEMY I'VE EVER FACED.
A BLOODTHIRSTY CRIMINAL WITH NO CONCERN FOR THE INNOCENT PEOPLE HE KILLED--NOT IF THEY STOOD IN HIS WAY.
ONLY WITH KHAN BEHIND BARS DID I FEEL FREE TO LEAVE THE COUNTRY AND RESUME MY STUDIES AND MEDITATION.
ONE OF THE DEADLIEST MEN ALIVE, LOCKED AWAY FOR THE REST OF HIS LIFE.
HE BELIEVES HE IS DESCENDED FROM GENGHIS KHAN, THAT HE IS BORN TO CONQUER AND TO RULE. COULD HE HAVE FOUND A WAY TO ASSERT HIS INFLUENCE FROM BEHIND MAXIMUM SECURITY?
KHAN'S BEEN IN SOLITARY FOR MORE THAN TWO DECADES. I WILL BE THE FIRST VISITOR HE HAS EVER RECEIVED.
THE CRANSTON NAME STILL HAS SOME CLOUT, AND I WAS ABLE TO MAKE A FEW CALLS TO GET IN.
THE QUESTION IS: AM I WASTING MY TIME? AM I BEING PLAYED AGAIN?
HE RECEIVES NO VISITORS AND NO COMMUNICATION INSIDE OR OUT. HE GETS BOOKS IN THE MAIL--PAPERBACK ONLY--BUT THAT'S IT. THEY'RE MOSTLY RELIGIOUS OR PHILOSOPHICAL IN NATURE.
I KNOW WHAT HE DID YEARS BEFORE, BUT I CAN TELL YOU THAT, FOR US, HE'S A MODEL PRISONER.
I DON'T KNOW WHAT YOU'RE LOOKING FOR, BUT I DOUBT YOU'LL FIND IT HERE.

YOU HAVE NOT AGED. YOU HAVE MASTERED THE TECHNIQUES OF SHAMBHALA.
AND YOU ARE AN OLD MAN. IS THAT WHY YOU ARE STRIKING BACK NOW? IS THIS PURE SPITE?
I COULD READ NEWS OF THE OUTSIDE WORLD IF I WISHED, BUT I DO NOT. CONSEQUENTLY, I CAN ONLY GUESS AT YOUR MEANING.
PERHAPS IT WILL BE HARD FOR YOU TO BELIEVE, BUT MY INCARCERATION IS THE BEST THING THAT COULD HAVE HAPPENED TO ME. AT LAST I HAVE FOUND SOME MEASURE OF PEACE.
HOW NICE FOR YOU. WHAT ABOUT THE FAMILIES OF THE PEOPLE YOU'VE KILLED? WHERE IS THEIR PEACE?
I MUST LIVE WITH THE KNOWLEDGE OF MY CRIMES. THAT IS MY BURDEN, AND I DO NOT RUN FROM IT.
GIVE ME A BREAK.
YOU'RE TELLING ME YOU'VE GOT NOTHING TO DO WITH THIS CURRENT CRIME WAVE?
MY NETWORK DISBANDED AFTER MY ARREST. I HAVE NO CONTACT WITH THE WORLD OUTSIDE THESE WALLS. I AM CONTENT WITH THAT.
YOU'RE CONTENT WITH GROWING OLD AND DYING IN PRISON?
I AM.
THE QUESTION YOU MUST ASK IS IF YOU ARE CONTENT TO REMAIN YOUNG?
IN SHAMBHALA WE LEARN TO MANIPULATE THE ENERGY OF THE UNIVERSE TO PROLONG OUR YOUTH. HERE, LOCKED AWAY FROM THE WORLD, I HAVE LEARNED TO GROW AND EVOLVE. I HAVE, AT LONG LAST, CHANGED.
NOT YOU. YOU APPEAR THE SAME. SO MANY YEARS HAVE PASSED, BUT YOU ASSUME THE SAME BURDENS. YOU ARE A RELIC OF A DIFFERENT TIME, RAGING AGAINST A WORLD THAT HAS PASSED YOU BY. HOW CAN YOU EVER KNOW PEACE?

I DON'T HAVE TIME FOR THIS. PEOPLE ARE GETTING KILLED OUT THERE, AND IF YOU'RE BEHIND IT, I'LL FIND OUT.
LET GO OF THE PAST. YOU MUST EMBRACE CHANGE.
ONLY BY EMBRACING CHANGE WILL YOU COME TO FIND MEANING.
YOU KEEP ON TELLING YOURSELF THAT. YOU'RE PATHETIC. AN AGING MURDERER WHO IS TRYING TO MAKE SENSE OF A LIFE IN PRISON.
PERHAPS YOU ARE RIGHT. TIME WILL TELL.
ARE YOU ALRIGHT, MR. CRANSTON? PRISONER SHOOK YOU UP?
NO, I'M FINE. I DON'T KNOW. JUST A LITTLE DIZZY.
DID YOU FIND WHAT YOU WERE LOOKING FOR?
I DIDN'T FIND ANYTHING. I WAS WASTING MY TIME.

"DID YOU LEARN ANYTHING, CRANSTON?"
"IT WAS A DEAD END, MAVIS."
AS NEAR AS I CAN TELL, EVERYTHING WE'VE DONE HAS BEEN A WASTE OF TIME.
I ESTABLISHED THIS NETWORK BEFORE I LEFT THE COUNTRY SO THIS SORT OF THING WOULDN'T HAPPEN. SOME CREEP IS RUNNING RINGS AROUND US AND WE'RE OFF CHASING GHOSTS.
I THOUGHT I COULD COUNT ON YOU TO GET THINGS DONE.
EVERYTHING THAT CAN BE DONE IS BEING DONE, MR. CRANSTON.
I KNOW IT'S FRUSTRATING, AND I CAN'T EXPLAIN WHY WE HAVEN'T FOUND ANYTHING, BUT IT'S NOT FOR WANT OF EFFORT.
BUT I WONDER IF IT IS THE RIGHT KIND OF EFFORT.
KYLE, IS THIS REALLY THE TIME TO TRY TO PULL A POWER PLAY? JUST DO YOUR DAMN JOB AND I'LL WORRY ABOUT MINE.
UNFORTUNATELY, MY JOB IS TO POINT OUT WHEN YOU'RE NOT DOING YOURS.
IF YOU CAN'T HANDLE THE JOB, MAVIS--
WHO THE HELL DO YOU THINK YOU ARE? YOU ARE OFF DOING GOD KNOWS WHAT IN SOME HIDDEN TIBETAN BEAUTY SPA FOR DECADES, WHILE I'M HERE DOING YOUR JOB. AND NOW YOU COME BACK ASKING WHY I HAVEN'T DONE MORE?
AND KYLE, I DON'T KNOW WHO YOU THINK YOU'RE FOOLING, BUT THE FACT THAT YOUR GRANDFATHER WAS AN AGENT IS ONLY GOING TO GET YOU SO FAR IN THIS ORGANIZATION. IT SURE AS HELL ISN'T GOING TO GET YOU INTO MY CHAIR.
NOW, BOTH OF YOU GET OUT OF MY OFFICE.

OCKHART
I NEED Ms. LOCKHART.
IT'S AGENT FORSYTHE. SHE'S IN A COMPROMISED SITUATION AND NEEDS A *WET WORK* AGENT, BUT THEY'RE ALL IN THE FIELD.
FORSYTHE, HUH?
LET ME HANDLE THIS.
GIVE ME THE DETAILS. I CAN GET THE WORD TO SOMEONE WHO CAN HELP.
MARGO FORSYTHE IS THE GRANDDAUGHTER OF MARGO LANE, WHO WAS MY BEST GIRL WAY BACK WHEN.
MARGO LANE IS LONG GONE, BUT MARGO FORSYTHE IS A DEAD RINGER. I'VE BEEN LOOKING FOR A CHANCE TO GET TO KNOW HER.
HOW DID I GET MYSELF INTO THIS?
I DON'T KNOW, DOLL, BUT I LOOK FORWARD TO HEARING THE STORY.

SO THE ***MAN HIMSELF*** FINALLY SHOWS HIS FACE. OR PART OF IT. I HEARD ALL ABOUT YOU FROM MY GRANDMOTHER.

SHE RESENTED THE FACT THAT SHE GREW OLD AND I DIDN'T, BUT I ALWAYS CARED FOR HER.

DIDN'T STOP YOU FROM RUNNING OFF, DID IT?

HE'S IN THERE. THIS IS IT. LET'S MOVE!

THIS IS A ***SET-UP!***

YOU ***THINK?***

I DON'T HAVE THE TRAINING FOR THIS! THEY SENT ME HERE TO RETRIEVE PHONE RECORDS.

RELAX. THIS IS WHAT I DO BEST.

MY ABILITY TO CLOUD THEIR MINDS WILL MAKE IT IMPOSSIBLE FOR THEM TO HURT US.

SOMEONE CLEARLY CLOUDED MY ***JUDGMENT*** WHEN I TOOK THIS JOB.

THAT IS SO LAME....

SO MUCH FOR HE ABILITY TO CLOUD MEN'S MINDS.
SOMETHING IS NOT RIGHT....
BUT I STILL HAVE A FEW TRICKS UP MY SLEEVE.
WE'VE LOST THEM.
SO FAR, I'M NOT IMPRESSED WITH THE LEGEND.
I SAVED YOUR LIFE, DIDN'T I MISS LANE?
IT'S Ms. FORSYTHE. AND BARELY.
THESE MEN ARE DEADLY, BUT NOT PARTICULARLY SKILLED. GETTING OUT OF HERE SHOULD NOT BE TOO HARD.
STILL, THAT DOESN'T EXPLAIN WHY I'M OFF MY GAME. I HAVEN'T FELT RIGHT ALL DAY.
THEY GOT TO ME TOO EASILY.
IT'S A CODE 5-181. I HAVE TO GO.
WHAT IS A 5-181?
IT MEANS EVERYONE RETURNS TO BASE.
IT'S YOUR ORGANIZATION. YOU OUGHT TO KNOW THE DAMN CODES.

EVERYONE RETURN TO BASE. WHAT CAN THAT BE ABOUT?

IT SEEMED WISEST TO RETURN AS CRANSTON.

AMELIA, WHAT'S HAPPENING?

NOTHING. AS FAR AS I KNOW WHY?

WHAT'S THIS ABOUT A 5-181? I DIDN'T ORDER THAT COMMAND.

I DID.

SHIWAN KHAN ESCAPED

I THOUGHT IT MIGHT BE A GOOD IDEA, IN LIGHT OF THIS.

YOUR OLD PAL KHAN HAS ESCAPED.

I KNEW IT.

WAIT A MINUTE. IF YOU ISSUED A 5-181, THEN WHY AREN'T AGENTS CHECKING IN?

BECAUSE THEY'RE *DEAD*, JUST LIKE YOU.

REALLY, I NEVER BELIEVED WE WOULD BE ABLE TO TRICK YOU SO EASILY.
OUR GOLDEN MASTER, SHIWAN KHAN SAID YOUR ARROGANCE WOULD MAKE YOU PLIABLE. NOW YOU WILL PAY THE PRICE FOR THAT ARROGANCE. ALL OVER THE CITY, YOUR AGENTS ARE FALLING.
"FOR LONGER THAN YOU WOULD BELIEVE, OUR AGENTS HAVE OUTNUMBERED THE FEW LOYAL SHADOW AGENTS.
"WE WAITED ONLY FOR THE MASTER TO GIVE THE WORD.
BANG
"IT ALL HAPPENED UNDER YOUR NOSE, MAVIS. I TRIED TO TELL YOU THAT YOU WERE SLIPPING.
"IT WOULD HAVE BEEN EASIER IF I COULD HAVE CONVINCED YOU TO STEP ASIDE, BUT IN THE END IT IS ALL THE SAME.
"ALL WE NEEDED WAS FOR YOU, CRANSTON, TO VISIT KHAN IN PRISON. HE NEEDED PROXIMITY TO YOU TO SUMMON THE ENERGY TO ESCAPE.
"WE BAITED THE TRAP, AND YOU WALKED RIGHT INTO IT."
YOU'RE INSANE. DO YOU THINK YOU CAN TRY TO PULL THIS OFF HERE, OF ALL PLACES?
TWO DO-GOODERS AND A HOSTAGE AGAINST ME? AND A TEAM OF MASTER KHAN'S AGENTS OUTSIDE THAT DOOR? YEAH, I REALLY DO.
WE'VE ANTICIPATED YOUR EVERY MOVE SO FAR. WHAT DO YOU THINK YOU CAN COME UP WITH NOW THAT WILL SURPRISE US?

NOW LET'S JUST TAKE IT EASY, KYLE. NO ONE HAS TO GET HURT.
THAT'S RIGHT. NO ONE HAS TO GET HURT. AS LONG AS YOU COME WITH ME. IF *YOU'RE* MY HOSTAGE, AND I CAN BRING YOU TO THE MASTER, THEN THESE TWO CAN GO.
SURE. YOU GOT IT. JUST LET THE WOMEN LEAVE.
DAMN IT. I DID LET THINGS GET AWAY FROM ME. BUT THIS IS STILL MY COMMAND, AND I WILL NOT ALLOW YOU TO BE BROUGHT TO KHAN LIKE A *PRIZE*.
I DON'T THINK YOU HAVE MUCH OF A *CHOICE*.
THINK *AGAIN*.
NO!

WE'RE OUTNUMBERED! WHAT ARE YOU DOING?
YOU ARE GOING TO HAVE TO TRUST ME.
IT'S NOT THAT I EVER ANTICIPATED THIS HAPPENING. NOT REALLY. BUT I ALWAYS THOUGHT IT BEST TO BE PREPARED.
BANG
BANG BANG
I'VE BEEN HIT. NO TIME TO FIGURE OUT HOW BAD.
THIS ESCAPE CHUTE WORKS ITS WAY THROUGH SEVERAL BUILDINGS ON THIS BLOCK. IT WILL TAKE THEM HOURS TO TRACE IT.
FIND OUT WHERE THAT GOES! THE MASTER WANTS HIM. FIND HIM!
BY THAT TIME, WE'LL BE LONG GONE....
...EITHER THAT, OR I'LL BE LONG DEAD.

LATER...
I WOULD HAVE PREFERRED TO HAVE MY OLD ENEMY DRAGGED BEFORE ME, BUT IN THE END IT DOES NOT MATTER.
YOU HAVE DONE WELL, KYLE VINCENT.
THE MAN WHO POSED THE GREATEST *THREAT* TO MY RETURN HAS, INSTEAD, *FACILITATED* IT.
EVEN IF HE LIVES, HE WILL FIND HIS POWER DIMINISHED, HIS ALLIES DEAD, HIS ASSETS STOLEN, HIS SAFE-HOUSES COMPROMISED. HIS *NETWORK* LIES IN *RUINS*.
THE *SHADOW* HAS *FADED*.
THE ERA OF KHAN HAS BEGUN.

SSUE #2 COVER

AFTER YEARS IN THE EAST, IN THE MYSTICAL FORTRESS OF *SHAMBHALA*, I HAVE RETURNED TO NEW YORK. I PLANNED TO TAKE UP THE MANTLE OF THE *SHADOW* ONCE MORE, AND WITH THE AID OF MY NETWORK, FIGHT THE FORCES OF EVIL.
THAT PLAN'S PRETTY MUCH DOWN THE CRAPPER.
RED HOOK HARDWARE
CLEARANCE SALE!!!
THE NETWORK IS GONE, INFILTRATED AND DESTROYED BY MY OLDEST ENEMY, SHIWAN KHAN. I'VE BEEN SHOT. I HAVE ONLY ONE ALLY LEFT--MARGO FORSYTHE, THE GRANDDAUGHTER OF MY OLD FLAME, MARGO LANE.
SHE ISN'T HAPPY TO BE PART OF THE TEAM, BUT I'M GUESSING SHE PREFERS IT TO BEING DEAD.

WE'VE GOT ASSASSINS AFTER US AND NO RESOURCES. MARGO HATES BEING STUCK WITH ME, BUT DOESN'T DARE STRIKE OUT ALONE.
I'LL GIVE HER THIS: SHE MAKES THE BEST OF IT AND DOES HER DUTY.
YOU'D MAKE A FINE NURSE. ALL YOU NEED IS THE UNIFORM.
GOD, YOU'RE SUCH A RELIC. THEY ACTUALLY ALLOW WOMEN TO BE DOCTORS NOW.
AND LAWYERS TOO, FROM WHAT I HEAR. WHERE WILL IT END?
SHE LOOKS SO MUCH LIKE HER GRANDMOTHER WHEN SHE WAS YOUNG, BUT SHE'S AN ENTIRELY DIFFERENT PERSON. I HAVE TO MAKE SURE I REMEMBER THAT.
AND SHE'S GOT SKILLS OF HER OWN.
THE PREVIOUS NIGHT.
WITH NO MONEY AND NO FRIENDS, SHE STILL FOUND A WAY TO GET ME ANTIBIOTICS. SHE SAVED MY LIFE. MAYBE A LITTLE GRUDGINGLY, BUT SHE DID IT.
SHE THREW HER LOT IN WITH THE SHADOW AGENCY. MAYBE SHE THOUGHT SHE HAD TO BECAUSE OF WHO HER GRANDMOTHER WAS. MAYBE SHE WANTED TO UNDERSTAND HER PAST.
WHATEVER SHE WAS LOOKING FOR, IT WASN'T A LIFE OF POVERTY, HIDING OUT IN A CHEAP MOTEL IN ONE OF THE WORST NEIGHBORHOODS IN THE CITY.

DELI
$19.54, HONEY.
PRICES ARE A LITTLE HIGH, DON'T YOU THINK?
YOU WANT CHEAP GROCERIES, GO TO WHERE THE RICH FOLK LIVE.
GIVEN THE SIZE OF THE CRANSTON FORTUNE, IT SHOULDN'T BE THIS WAY, BUT KHAN IS CLEVER AND RUTHLESS.

HE'S GOTTEN THE BANKS TO BELIEVE THEY CAN FORECLOSE ON MY PROPERTIES. MARGO SAYS HE'S "HACKED" INTO THE BANK'S COMPUTER. WHATEVER THAT MEANS.
I KNOW THIS MUCH-- IT MEANS WE'RE BROKE.
CARD DENIED
WE HAVE NOWHERE TO GO AND NO RESOURCES TO STRENGTHEN OUR POSITION. IT'S BAD.

THIS IS MY STORE. GET OUT OF HERE BEFORE I CALL THE COPS.
COPS AIN'T COMING, BITCH.

YOU HEAR THAT? SOMEONE'S STANDING UP TO THOSE *HOODS* WE'VE SEEN AROUND HERE. HE'S IN *TROUBLE*.
WE'RE IN TROUBLE. I'LL CALL THE POLICE. THEY'LL DEAL WITH IT. IT'S THEIR JOB.
ARE YOU *REALLY* GOING TO TRY TO PLAY THE *HERO?* YOU CAN BARELY MOVE.
YOU'VE LOST EVERYTHING BECAUSE MY ENEMY WANTED TO KEEP ME FROM DOING WHAT I DO. I CAN'T LET THAT HAPPEN.
AND HOW IS YOUR GETTING YOURSELF *KILLED* GOING TO HELP ME?
IF I'M KILLED, NO ONE WILL BOTHER TO HUNT YOU DOWN.
MAYBE I WAS A LITTLE HARSH, BUT--
OKAY, MAYBE HE'S A *LITTLE* IMPRESSIVE.

DERRICK, YOU ALWAYS WERE STRANGE, BUT NOW FOR REAL YOU MUST BE OUT OF YOUR MIND. THAT'S WHAT I THINK.
MAN IS CRAZY.
RUNNING OUR BOY OFF. WHAT IS THAT?
YOUR BOY WAS DEALING RIGHT IN FRONT OF MY STORE.
MIGHT BE YOUR STORE, BUT IT'S OUR SIDEWALK. AND NOW YOU GOT TO PAY UP. COMPENSATE US FOR WHAT WE LOST.
I KNOW YOUR MAMA, BOY. SHE'S A GOOD LADY. HOW DO YOU THINK SHE'D FEEL TO SEE YOU LIKE THIS.
I'M TAKING CARE OF BUSINESS. THAT'S HOW SHE RAISED ME.
SHE DIDN'T RAISE YOU TO RUIN YOUR OWN NEIGHBORHOOD. YOU'RE CRAPPING WHERE YOU EAT, SON.
I HEARD ENOUGH. NOW YOU ARE GOING TO TAKE US INSIDE AND OPEN THAT SAFE, OR I'M GOING TO DROP YOU RIGHT HERE. I AIN'T GOING TO TELL YOU AGAIN.

WHAT THE HELL IS THAT?
TIME TO PAY THE PRICE FOR YOUR INIQUITY.
FOR HIS *WHAT?*
CRIME DOESN'T PAY, SON.
YOU ARE ONE CORNY-ASS VIGILANTE. LET'S SEE YOU SO I CAN SHOOT YOU.
CRACK

ARE YOU HURT?
NO, I'M OKAY.
RETURN TO YOUR ESTABLISHMENT AND PHONE THE AUTHORITIES. THEY'LL REMOVE YOUR ASSAILANTS.
POLICE DON'T COME OUT HERE. I'M SURPRISED TO SEE ONE OF YOUR KIND.
WAIT A MINUTE. ARE YOU *ROLLING* THIS GUY?
DESPERATE TIMES...
THEY'RE ABOUT TO GET *MORE* DESPERATE.
COMMERCIAL PHOTOGRA
"YOU DIDN'T THINK THERE WERE ONLY THREE OF THEM, DID YOU?"

I'D HOPED TO DEAL WITH THIS NON-VIOLENTLY, BUT I GUESS THAT'S NOT GOING TO HAPPEN.
IT RARELY DOES.
RATT-TATT-TATT-TATT
COME ON OUT OF THERE. YOU GOT OPTION A) YOU THROW DOWN THE GUNS AND PUT YOUR HANDS UP. AND YOU GOT OPTION B)YOU GET SHOT.
OR SOME CHICK IS GOING TO KICK YOUR ASSES FROM ABOVE. THAT'S OPTION C.
THUD

WHAT'S YOUR NAME?
DERRICK.
OKAY, DERRICK. YOU'RE HIRED. WELCOME TO THE SHADOW NETWORK.
DON'T WORRY. WE'LL BE IN TOUCH.
WHERE DID HE GO?
IT'S WHY THEY CALL HIM THE SHADOW.
HE'S LESS A MAN THAN A FORCE OF NATURE.
NO ONE EVEN KNOWS IF HE IS TRULY HUMAN.
YOU CAN ONLY KNOW THAT HE IS AS MUCH TO BE FEARED AS RESPECTED.

FIVE MINUTES LATER.
FORCE OF NATURE MY ASS.
THAT WAS STUPID.
STUPID. BUT FUN. CHANGE OF CLOTHES OVER THERE. NO *PEEKING*.
WHAT, YOU HAVE TO PROVE YOU'RE STILL A *MAN?*
THE PEOPLE OF THIS NEIGHBORHOOD NEED A PROTECTOR. BESIDES, I GOT SOME CASH OUT OF IT. AND WE HAVE A *RECRUIT*. WE'RE NOT GOING TO DEFEAT KHAN WITHOUT A NEW NETWORK.
I STILL THINK IT WAS STUPID. THOUGH KIND OF *IMPRESSIVE*.
YOU WEREN'T BAD YOURSELF.
DON'T GO THINKING WE'RE *FRIENDS* NOW.
NEVER.
I REALLY HOPE YOU ARE NOT ATTEMPTING TO *FLIRT* WITH ME.
WOULDN'T DREAM OF IT.

UPPER
EAST SIDE
KYLE, WHAT
WORD OF OUR
QUARRY?
MY KHAN, I AM FOLLOWING UP ON A LEAD RIGHT NOW WITH THIS CAB DRIVER.
WE ESTABLISHED YOU GAVE A RIDE TO A BEAUTIFUL YOUNG GIRL AND A WOUNDED MAN. ***WHERE*** DID YOU TAKE THEM?
I TOLD YOU. I DON'T REMEMBER. SOME BAD MOTEL, BUT I DON'T KNOW WHICH ONE.
DO YOU REMEMBER NOW?
NO, PLEASE DON'T! I CAN'T REMEMB-- ***AHHHHH!***

HOW'S THE MEMORY COMING ALONG?
HE TOLD ME NOT TO TELL, BUT IT WAS IN THE BRONX. THE BRONX...THE HUNTS POINT MOTEL.
SEE, THAT WASN'T SO HARD, WAS IT?
THAT'S A BIG TIP FOR TAKING YOU TO THE CRAPPIEST MOTEL IN BROOKLYN.
WE ARE IN THE BRONX. IF ANYONE ASKS, WE'RE IN THE BRONX.
YEAH. WHAT I MEANT. THE BRONX. WHAT'S WRONG WITH ME?
THE BRONX... THE BRONX...
THANKS FOR EVERYTHING.
NO!
CRACK
IN THE MATTER OF LOCATING MR. CRANSTON'S LOCATION, WE ARE MAKING CONSIDERABLE PROGRESS.
I AM PLEASED

OUR NEXT STEP IS CONVINCING THE MAJOR CRIME ORGANIZATIONS IN NEW YORK TO DEDICATE A PERCENTAGE OF THEIR EARNINGS TO US.
A *CLASSIC* MOVE, MY KHAN.
YES, AND IT IS SOMETHING OUR ENEMY KNOWS A GREAT DEAL ABOUT. MORE THAN EVER, I NEED HIM OUT OF THE WAY.
MY KHAN, IF I MAY INQUIRE...YOU HAVE MANAGED TO ACCUMULATE *SIGNIFICANT* WEALTH, AND THE AUTHORITIES CAN'T LINK YOU TO IT. THEY HAVE NO IDEA WHO YOU ARE. WHY TAKE THE RISK?
THERE IS NO RISK. THESE ANIMALS WILL EARN MONEY, AND WE WILL TAKE IT FROM THEM.
BUT TO WHAT END? IT WOULD HELP IF I UNDERSTOOD THE END GAME. IS IT MORE WEALTH YOU WANT? MORE ***POWER?***
WHEN YOU'VE BEEN ALIVE AS LONG AS I HAVE, THERE ARE TWO THINGS THAT BECOME PREOCCUPATIONS. ***LONGEVITY*** AND ***LEGACY.***
I HAVE AGED IN PRISON. USING THE TECHNIQUES I MASTERED IN SHAMBHALA, I CAN SLOW FURTHER AGING, BUT I CANNOT ***REVERSE*** THE PROCESS.
SO AS TO THE FIRST OF MY CONCERNS, LONGEVITY. I WISH TO REGAIN MY ***YOUTH***. THAT IS WHY I BUILT THIS.

WOW.
I HAVE THE MEANS TO CONDUCT ADVANCED EXPERIMENTATION. I BELIEVE I CAN, BY COMBINING THE KNOWLEDGE OF THE EAST AND THE WEST, DISCOVER THE KEY TO REVERSING THE AGING PROCESS.
BUT RUNNING THIS EQUIPMENT, AND THE RAW MATERIALS THEMSELVES, WILL BE MORE EXPENSIVE THAN YOU CAN IMAGINE. I NEED WEALTH.
LONGEVITY. CHECK. I GET IT. SO WHAT ABOUT LEGACY?
YOU WILL SEE TO THAT TOMORROW. THERE IS SOMEONE YOU MUST CONTACT, BUT YOU WILL HAVE TO BE ON YOUR GUARD. READ HER FILE CAREFULLY. YOU WILL SEE SHE MAY BE AMONG THE MOST *DANGEROUS* TARGETS I HAVE EVER DIRECTED YOU TOWARD.
WHO IS SHE?
A *TEENAGER.*

I'D LIKE TO RETURN THIS.
SURE. OF COURSE. ABSOLUTELY. DO YOU HAVE A RECEIPT?
TAKE AN EXTRA 20% off
CLEARANCE MERCHANDISE 20%
25% off ALL CITIZE- BULOVA WAT
terrific clearanc SALE
AS YOU CAN SEE, THE NECKLACE IS IN PERFECT SHAPE, AND THE RECEIPT SAYS I BOUGHT IT ONLY YESTERDAY. FOR $500. YOU CAN SEE THAT.
YEAH, I CAN SEE THAT. THIS ALL LOOKS RIGHT.
CAN I SHOW YOU ANYTHING ELSE?
MAYBE ANOTHER TIME, CUTIE.
HEY, WAIT A NUTE...THAT'S NOT RIGHT...
SECURITY. YEAH, I'D LIKE TO REPORT A HYPNOSIS.

COME ON. IT'S JUST $500. YOU'RE NOT GOING TO MISS IT.
AND MY **FREE PERIOD** IS ALMOST OVER. IF YOU MAKE ME LATE FOR **TRIGONOMETRY**, I'M GOING TO BE PISSED OFF. BECAUSE IF THERE'S ONE THING I LOVE...
IT'S TRIGONOMETRY.
NYPD! FREEZE.
GIVE ME A **BREAK!** ISN'T THAT ENOUGH PURSUIT FOR ONE DAY?
GET IN!
WHA....
HEY!
4 KAHN
SCREECH

UNLOCK THE DOORS AND LET ME OUT OF HERE, YOU PERV. BELIEVE ME, I'VE FACED WORSE THAN YOU, AND THEY DIDN'T ESCAPE WITH THEIR DICKS STILL WIRED TO THEIR BODIES.
RELAX, BATU. I'M ON YOUR SIDE.
HOW DO YOU KNOW MY NAME?
I KNOW A LOT ABOUT YOU, BATU KHAN. MORE THAN YOU KNOW ABOUT YOURSELF. YOU KNOW THAT YOU'RE AN ORPHAN, AND NO INFORMATION ABOUT YOUR FAMILY EXISTS. EXCEPT I HAVE THAT INFORMATION.
OKAY, CREEP. YOU ARE GOING TO TELL THE DRIVER TO STOP, AND YOU ARE GOING TO UNLOCK THE DOORS. THIS IS SOMETHING YOU WANT TO DO. YOU NEED TO DO IT.
THESE AREN'T THE DROIDS WE'RE LOOKING FOR. YEAH, YEAH. I'VE LEARNED HOW TO RESIST HYPNOSIS FROM THE ABSOLUTE MASTER, SO DON'T EVEN BOTHER.
WHERE ARE YOU TAKING ME?
TO MEET THAT MASTER, AND TO SEE THE MAN IN ACTION. IF YOUR FILE PAINTS AN ACCURATE PICTURE OF YOU, I THINK YOU'LL ENJOY THIS.
AND WHY IS THAT?
BECAUSE HE'S YOUR GRANDFATHER, AND HE'S THE TERRIFYING MONSTER YOU WISH YOU WERE.

SO, YOU'RE TELLING ME MY GRANDFATHER IS THAT KHAN, THE NOTORIOUS CRIMINAL.
THE CELEBRATED MASTERMIND. YES.
AND YOU ARE TAKING ME TO A MEETING OF GANG LORDS HE'S SET UP?
YES.
THIS IS GOING TO BE EPIC.
TWENTY PERCENT OF ALL PROFITS WILL COME TO ME. YOU WILL MAKE YOUR BOOKS AVAILABLE TO INSPECTION. THIS IS NOT NEGOTIABLE.
NO, IT'S BULLSHIT.
LEUNG IS RIGHT. I CAME HERE OUT OF CURIOSITY. YOU ARE FAMOUS, KHAN, FROM HISTORY BOOKS, BUT YOUR FAME IS WORTH NOTHING TO US. I WILL SHOW MY SON, DMITRY, HOW I SCORN SUCH THREATS.
YOU LOVE YOUR SON?
OF COURSE.

THEN KILL HIM. STRANGLE HIM.
I WON'T. I WILL NOT HURT MY SON. HOW DARE YOU THINK....
AHCH... AHCH...
I WILL NOT DO IT...

I WON'T... I WON'T...
TWENTY PERCENT SOUNDS GOOD TO ME.
I'M IN.
YEAH, WE'RE GOOD FOR THAT.
I WAS FOR PAYING ALL ALONG. THAT'S WHAT I SAID, GUYS, RIGHT? YOU *HEARD* ME SAY IT.
THANK YOU ALL FOR COMING. I LOOK FORWARD TO DOING BUSINESS.
KYLE HAS EXPLAINED EVERYTHING TO YOU. BATU, YOU ARE MY ONLY LIVING *RELATIVE*. I UNDERSTAND YOU SHOW SOME OF THE FAMILY *TALENT*. YOU HAVE SEEN WHAT I CAN DO, SO NOW I ASK, DO YOU WISH TO LEARN MORE?
HELLS, YEAH.

WITH BATU IN KHAN'S CARE, NOW WE ONLY HAVE TO FINISH ONE MAJOR TASK. *KILLING* CRANSTON.
AND HERE IT IS. THE DATES MATCH UP.
REGISTRATION
BANG
BANG BANG
BANG
DAMN CABBIE. I SHOULD HAVE LEFT HIM ALIVE. ALRIGHT, TIME TO FIGURE THIS OUT...

HOURS LATER.
SHOCKING NEWS TONIGHT FROM THE BRONX.
RED HOOK MOTEL
RED HOOK
AN ELDERLY COUPLE GUNNED DOWN IN THEIR BEDS IN A BRONX MOTEL ROOM...
THAT IS US.
THEY WERE LOOKING FOR US. PEOPLE ARE DEAD BECAUSE WE'RE HIDING OUT.
SO, WHAT ARE YOU SUGGESTING?
THAT WE DON'T HIDE ANY MORE.
YOU'RE IN LUCK.

LOOKS LIKE YOU'VE BEEN *FOUND*.

ISSUE #3 COVER

IT WAS ONLY A MATTER OF TIME BEFORE KYLE VINCENT, KHAN'S HENCHMAN, FOUND ME. HE MASTERMINDED THE DESTRUCTION OF THE SHADOW NETWORK, AND NOW HE MEANS TO FINISH THE JOB.

I'D BEEN CAREFUL TO COVER MY TRACKS, BUT KYLE IS GOOD. THOROUGH.

MY KHAN HAS ACCOMPLISHED SO MUCH IN HIS LIFE, BUT NOW IT'S TIME FOR ME TO DO THE ONE THING HE FAILED AT.

BANG

BANG

BANG

I'M RECOVERING FROM WOUNDS. I'M NOT AT MY BEST. BUT I'VE GOT TO PROTECT MARGO.

BANG BANG

FINALLY. THE END OF THE SHADOW!

BANG

BANG

BANG

MANY HAVE TRIED AND PAID FOR THEIR ARROGANCE. SOON YOU SHALL JOIN THEM.
HA HA HA HA HA HA HA
BANG
YOU SHOULD WORRY MORE ABOUT DRAWING ME OUT.
BANG
NG
IT'S LIKE HE'S VANISHING AND REAPPEARING.
GET THE WOMAN. THAT WILL DRAW HIM OUT.
I CAN'T GET A FIX ON HIM.
DAMN IT!
BLAM!
BLAM!
BLAM

I SUPPOSE YOU'RE GOING TO WANT TO *INTERROGATE* ME. I'VE GOT NEWS FOR YOU. YOU'RE NOT GOING TO GET ANYTHING. I'VE BEEN TRAINED BY MY *KHAN*. I'LL DIE FIRST.

PRETTY MUCH WHAT I FIGURED.

YOU HAVE A PROBLEM WITH THAT?

NONE.

DAMN.

EVEN IN THIS NEIGHBORHOOD, THE COPS ARE GOING TO HAVE TO SHOW UP AFTER A SHOOTOUT. WE NEED TO SCRAM.
WHERE ARE WE GOING TO GO, CRANSTON? THERE'S NO PLACE LEFT.
WE'LL GO TO MY LAST SAFE HOUSE. I HAD ONE BURIED SO DEEPLY EVEN KHAN COULDN'T FIND IT.
IF YOU HAD A SAFE HOUSE, WHAT THE HELL WERE WE DOING IN THIS FLEA BAG MOTEL?
THEY WERE ALWAYS GOING TO FIND US. I WAS INJURED AND WE COULDN'T PROPERLY COVER OUR TRACKS. WHEN THEY DID CATCH UP WITH US, I WANTED IT TO BE SOMEPLACE DISPOSABLE.
SO WE WERE OUR OWN BAIT? YOU MIGHT HAVE TOLD ME THAT.
IT MIGHT HAVE MADE YOU NERVOUS.
LOOK, MARGO, YOU'VE GOT TO ANTICIPATE YOUR ENEMY AND WORK AGAINST HIS NEXT MOVES. THAT'S WHAT I'M DOING. THAT'S WHAT I ALWAYS DO. THAT'S WHAT IS GOING TO KEEP US ALIVE LONG ENOUGH TO GET BACK TO FULL STRENGTH.

HOW ARE WE GOING TO GET TO THIS SAFE HOUSE WITHOUT DRAWING ATTENTION TO OURSELVES? IN A CAB? ON THE SUBWAY? PEOPLE WILL *SEE* US.
YOU MIGHT TELL ME WHAT YOU HAVE PLANNED.
I THOUGHT I'D TAKE THAT FORD TAURUS I PROCURED. DID YOU KNOW IT'S THE MOST *ANONYMOUS* CAR IN AMERICA?
TELLING YOU MAKES IT LOOK LESS *IMPRESSIVE* WHEN IT ALL COMES TOGETHER. NOW GRAB KYLE'S FEET. WE'VE GOT TO MOVE.
AND IF SOMEONE SEES US CARRYING A *CORPSE?*
"POWER TO CLOUD MEN'S MINDS." IT'S PRACTICALLY ON THE *BUSINESS CARD.*
WE'LL SEE HOW WELL THAT WORKS.
NICE EVENING, DON'T YOU THINK?
MIGHT RAIN.
GASP HEAVY.
IT IS THE WAY OF SCOUNDRELS.
SAVE THE THEATRICS FOR A MORE APPRECIATIVE AUDIENCE. WHY ARE WE EVEN TAKING THE BODY?
AS A WAY OF MAKING AMENDS, KYLE IS GOING TO DO ONE LAST FAVOR FOR US. HE IS GOING TO DELIVER A *MESSAGE*.

LATER THAT NIGHT.

HERE WE ARE.

EVENING, MA'AM. NICE NIGHT.

DON'T THINK IT'S LIKELY TO RAIN.

NEXT TIME, LET ME PICK THE NEIGHBORHOOD.

SQUEAK SQUEAK SQUEAK

OUR HOME FOR THE FORESEEABLE FUTURE.

IS IT TOO LATE TO GO BACK TO THE MOTEL?

SHIWAN KHAN'S UPPER EAST SIDE MANSION.
THE NEXT MORNING.
OH MY GOD, KAYLEIGH, YOU WOULDN'T BELIEVE THIS PLACE.
BATU KAHN. SHIWAN KHAN'S GRANDDAUGHTER.
I KNOW. IT'S CRAZY RIGHT? THE GRANDFATHER I NEVER KNEW I HAD SHOWS UP OUT OF NOWHERE. HE'S LOADED, AND TELLS ME I DON'T HAVE TO GO TO SCHOOL.
NO, HE EXPECTS ME TO DO THINGS, BUT THEY'RE COOL THINGS. HE'S TRAINING ME TO, LIKE, TAKE OVER HIS BUSINESS.
NO. BELIEVE ME. *DULL* IS THE LAST THING THIS PLACE IS.
YOUR MOVE
ACTUALLY, IT'S PRETTY *INTENSE*.

YOU TOLD ME YOU WANTED ME TO SHOW INITIATIVE. I'M HOPING CARRYING IN YOUR CORPSES COUNTS.
IT IS A GOOD START.
HE WAS, LIKE, YOUR BIG HENCHMAN, RIGHT?
YES. I FEAR YOU MAY NEED TO TAKE ON MORE RESPONSIBILITIES SOONER THAN I ANTICIPATED. I HAVE MANY UNDERLINGS BUT FEW I CAN TRUST ENTIRELY. DO YOU BELIEVE YOU ARE EQUAL TO THE TASK, MY GRAND-DAUGHTER?
JUST TELL ME WHAT TO DO.
YOU WILL NEED TO GET DRESSED, AND I WILL SHOW YOU MORE OF MY WORK. IN THE MEANTIME, PLEASE PUT THE CORPSE IN THE REMAINS-DISPOSAL INCINERATOR IN THE BASEMENT.
MY GRANDFATHER HAS AN INCINERATOR SPECIFICALLY FOR DISPOSING OF CORPSES. THAT IS SO COOL.

IDTOWN MANHATTAN.
ATER THAT DAY.
"THE TOP FLOORS BELONGED TO AN INVESTMENT HOUSE THAT WAS TOO BIG TO FAIL. THE LEASE WAS QUITE AFFORDABLE."
THIS IS NOW THE CENTER OF MY OPERATION.
WHAT IS ALL THIS?
THIS IS THE PURPOSE OF MY WORK.
WEALTH IN ITSELF IS MEANINGLESS. POWER IS WITHOUT PURPOSE UNLESS YOU HAVE POWER OVER WHAT MATTERS MOST.
AND WHAT MATTERS MOST?
FAMILY AND LEGACY.
IT IS WHY I FOUND YOU AND PLUCKED YOU OUT OF OBSCURITY.
BEYOND THAT, MY QUEST IS THE SECRET OF LIFE ITSELF. YOUTH. VITALITY. I AGED IN PRISON, AND I WANT RETURNED WHAT THE SHADOW STOLE FROM ME.
THAT IS THE PURPOSE OF MY WORK HERE. IT IS THE ENGINE WHICH OUR MONEY AND POWER FEED.
IT IS IN THE SERVICE OF THESE GOALS THAT YOU MUST APPLY YOURSELF TO LEARN AND GROW.

"YOU MUST PRACTICE YOUR FIGHTING SKILLS.
BANG BANG BANG
"BUT YOU MUST NOT NEGLECT MODERN WEAPONS.
"YOU MUST REFINE YOUR MYSTIC SKILLS."
EXCUSE ME, SIR, BUT YOU CANNOT BREATHE.
AHKKKKK
"IF YOU APPLY YOURSELF IN THESE THINGS, YOU WILL BE PREPARED TO EXECUTE ALL THE TASKS I ASK OF YOU."

GENTLEMEN, WE'RE SUPPOSED TO BE THE MOST DANGEROUS MEN IN THE CITY. THE MOST FEARED.
SO WHY ARE WE HANDING OVER OUR HARD-EARNED MONEY TO SOME FOSSIL? SHIWAN KHAN? A CLOWN WHO CLAIMS TO BE THE HEIR TO GENGHIS KHAN? HE'S A JOKE, AND WE LET HIM TREAT US LIKE A PUPPETEER WITH HIS HAND UP OUR ASSES.
HE FORCED IVAN TO KILL HIS OWN SON. ANY ONE OF US COULD BE NEXT. ARE YOU GOING TO TAKE IT? ARE WE GOING TO BE HUMILIATED BY AN OLD JOKE WITH DELUSIONS OF GRANDEUR?
I SAY WE'VE HAD ENOUGH.
THAT'S NOT SUCH A GREAT IDEA, MR. LEUNG. FOR REAL.

YOU BELONG TO KHAN.
KHAN HAS NO POWER OVER US. AND WE WILL NOT BE INTIMIDATED BY A ***CHILD!*** SHOULDN'T YOU BE IN YOUR ALGEBRA CLASS?
I THINK IVAN LEARNED WHAT KIND OF POWER KHAN HAS OVER YOU. ISN'T THAT RIGHT, IVAN?
YOU DON'T WANT TO LEARN THE SAME LESSON, DO YOU? YOU HAVE A SON AND A DAUGHTER, MR. LEUNG. WHICH WOULD YOU MOST HATE TO LOSE?
YOUR ***DAUGHTER?*** VERY TOUCHING, AND S
VERY UNTRADITIONAL.
I KNOW WHAT YOU ARE THINKING BEFORE YOU THINK IT. I KNEW ABOUT THIS MEETING, AND I WILL KNOW IF YOU HAVE ANOTHER. MY ADVICE TO YOU, GENTLEMEN--

DIE!
THAT FALLS UNDER THE HEADING OF KNOWING WHAT YOU'RE THINKING BEFORE YOU THINK IT. THAT WAS YOUR ONE **FREE PASS**. NEXT TIME IT WILL BE YOUR HEART.
AND YOUR **DAUGHTER'S** HEART, JUST FOR SPITE.
I EXPECT YOUR PAYMENTS TO BE ON TIME THIS WEEK. GOOD AFTERNOON, GENTS.

YES, I WANT REVENGE. BUT WHO IS THERE TO TAKE ON KHAN? YOU AND ME?
THE SHADOW SEES WHAT IS IN YOUR HEART. YOU DON'T WANT TO DIE. WHAT YOU WANT IS *REVENGE*.
YOU AND ME, FOR NOW.

"SOON THERE WILL BE MANY."
ARDWARE
CLEARANCE
OK
AND HERE'S YOUR CHANGE. THANKS SO MUCH.
RING RING RING
HELLO. YES. I UNDERSTAND. JUST TELL ME WHERE TO B AND WHEN TO BE THERE.

AMY. BABE. YOU'RE GOING TO HAVE TO WORK MORE HOURS. MAYBE WE'LL HIRE SOMEONE ELSE ON. BUT I HAVE OTHER THINGS I HAVE TO DO. I WON'T BE AROUND MUCH.
WHAT IS THIS ABOUT, DERICK? WHERE DO YOU HAVE TO GO? *WHO* WAS THAT ON THE PHONE?
IT'S AN *OBLIGATION*. I CAN'T TELL YOU MORE THAN THAT. YOU'LL HAVE TO MAKE DO. WE'LL MANAGE.
BUT WHAT ABOUT THOSE *THUGS* WHO'VE BEEN COMIN AROUND? YOU CAN'T EXPECT ME TO WORK HERE ALONE WITH THEM CAUSING TROUBLE.
I'VE BEEN TOLD THEY WON'T BE A PROBLEM.
HOW CA YOU KNO THAT?

"WHO IS GOING TO STOP THEM?"
COME ON, MAN. I ALMOST GOT ENOUGH.
ALMOST DOESN'T CUT IT. COME BACK IF YOU GOT THE GREEN.
DON'T DO ME LIKE THAT, PORKY. I WANT TO TALK TO FERRET.
NOTHING TO TALK ABOUT. UNLESS YOU HAVE THE MONEY, YOU DON'T GET THE PRODUCT. THAT'S WHAT IS KNOWN AS ECONOMICS.
THAT'S NO WAY TO TREAT A CUSTOMER. YOU'VE GONE CRAZY WITH POWER.
MAYBE SO, BUT YOU DON'T WANT TO SEE HOW CRAZY, NOW DO YOU?
I KNOW WHAT IS IN YOUR HEART, GERALD FERRIS.
THE HELL IS THAT? AND NO ONE CALLS ME GERALD.

GERALD FERRIS, THE CHOICE IS YOURS. YOU NEED NOT FOLLOW THE PATH OF EVIL.
YOU WANT ONLY *PURPOSE*.
I'LL SHOW YOU MY PURPOSE.
BANG, BANG, BANG
WHERE'D HE GO?
BANG BANG
I WANT PURPOSE. I'M *LOOKING* FOR PURPOSE REAL *HARD*.
SO BE IT. FROM THIS POINT ON, YOU SERVE THE SHADOW. YOU AND YOUR MEN WIL NO LONGER PURSUE EVIL BUT WILL BE A FORCE FOR GOOD.
AND I HAVE A *VITAL* TASK IN MIND FOR YOU.

"BATU, I AM
LEASED WITH YOUR
PROGRESS."
ALL OF THE SCUM IN OUR EMPLOY HAVE PAID WHAT THEY OWE. YOU HAVE KEPT THEM IN LINE NICELY.
I AIM TO PLEASE.
WATCH WHERE YOU'RE GOING.
PARDON ME, MA'AM. SIR.
COME. WE HAVE FAR MORE IMPORTANT THINGS TO TEND TO.

I MUST FOCUS MY ATTENTION ON MY WORK. I THEREFORE PRESENT YOU WITH A FINAL *TEST*.
YOU WANT ME TO *KILL* THE *SHADOW*.
I WOULD LIKE TO THINK MY MIND IS NOT OPEN TO YOU.
NO, BUT I FIGURED YOU'D ASK.
I'VE EVEN BEEN THINKING ABOUT HOW I MIGHT GO ABOUT IT. I SAY WE STRIKE THE SAME WAY YOU STRUCK BEFORE. AFTER ALL, IT WAS VERY EFFECTIVE.
WE TAKE HIM OUT FROM THE *INSIDE*

ATER THAT NIGHT
I KNOW HE'S, LIKE, ALL SCARY AND EVERYTHING, BUT I CAN ASSURE YOU, WE ARE MORE FRIGHTENING.
MORE IMPORTANTLY, WE HAVE A LOT TO OFFER.
HE'S PROMISING--WHAT?--A CHANCE AT REDEMPTION. I'VE GOT SOMETHING ELSE IN MIND.
A CHANCE TO GET *RICH*.
ALL YOU HAVE TO DO IS TELL US WHAT HE IS PLANNING FOR YOU.
HOW DOES THAT SOUND.

SOUNDS GOOD TO ME. YOU GIVE US THE BACKUP WE NEED AND THE SHADOW IS AS GOOD AS DEAD.

ISSUE #4 COVER
ART BY TIM BRADSTREET

ISSUE #4 COVER
ART BY COLTON WORLEY

MY OLDEST AND DEADLIEST ENEMY, SHIWAN KHAN, HAS *DESTROYED* THE *SHADOW NETWORK* AND *KILLED* NEARLY ALL OF THE OPERATIVES LOYAL TO THE CAUSE.
I'VE BEEN SHOT. I AM *WEAKENED* AND MY *POWERS* ARE *DIMINISHED*, BUT MY INTELLECT IS UNIMPAIRED.
KHAN MAKES HIS MOVES, BUT SO DO I. KHAN'S *OPENING* WAS DEVASTATING, BUT IT REMAINS TO BE SEEN WHO PLAYS A *BETTER* GAME.
KALUT

PORKY. A GANG LEADER AND DRUG DEALER. NOW PART OF THE SHADOW NETWORK.

STERANKO

DESPERATE TIMES CALL FOR A *LOWERING* OF STANDARDS.

WHAT WE GOT HERE?

BEAT DOWN!

CRACK

BE *COOL*, PORKY. NO NEED TO GET WORKED UP.

YOU GOT THE WORD, MAN. NO MORE MOVING *PRODUCT*. WE'RE KEEPING THESE STREETS *CLEAN* NOW. GOT A NEW BOSS, AND YOU KNOW WHAT THAT MEANS FOR YOU?

LISTEN UP, *BATU*. I'M NOT SAYING THERE'S NO MONEY TO BE MADE IN PRETENDING TO BE IN THE *SHADOW'S* CAMP, BUT IT AIN'T MUCH.

I CAN'T AFFORD TO PLAY GOOD GUY MUCH LONGER. I NEED *ACTION*.

SHIWAN KHAN'S MIDTOWN HEADQUARTERS
LEARN TO CHILL, PORKY. YOU'LL GET YOUR ACTION SOON ENOUGH.
WHILE I HIDE IN MY LAST REMAINING SAFE HOUSE, KHAN HAS SET UP HIS HEADQUARTERS, ESTABLISHED A LABORATORY, AND IS WORKING TOWARD AN UNKNOWN SCHEME.
SHIWAN KHAN
BATU KHAN
YOUR PROJECT MOVES FORWARD?
YES, GRANDFATHER. I HAVE IT UNDER CONTROL.
GOOD. I MUST DIRECT MY ENERGIES ELSEWHERE. WE ARE CLOSE. VERY CLOSE.
KHAN HAS ENTRUSTED HIS GRANDDAUGHTER WITH KILLING THE SHADOW. PERHAPS HE THINKS THAT, IN MY WEAKENED STATE, I AM NO MATCH FOR A TEENAGE GIRL. IT'S TRUE THAT I AM NOT BACK TO FULL STRENGTH, AND THIS IS NO ORDINARY TEENAGE GIRL.
WE ARE GOING TO NEED MASSIVE AMOUNTS OF ENERGY FOR THE NEXT PHASE, AND THAT MEANS A RELAY STATION. I WILL NEED MY BEST PEOPLE TO SECURE IT.
ARE YOU EVEN LISTENING TO ME?
REGULAR, WORTHLESS TEENAGERS CAN LISTEN TO AUTHORITY FIGURES AND TEXT AT THE SAME TIME. BUT I'VE GOT THE FAMILY MYSTIC POWERS, SO DON'T SWEAT IT.
HOW DO I KNOW ALL THIS?
THE LIST OF POSSIBLE RELAY STATIONS, MY KHAN. I BEG YOUR FORGIVENESS FOR NOT GETTING THIS TO YOU SOONER, BUT WE WANTED TO MAKE CERTAIN THERE WERE NO ERRORS.
ATTENTION TO DETAIL IS TO BE PRAISED IN AN AMERICAN.
BECAUSE I HAVE A MAN ON THE INSIDE.
DERICK ROSE, MEMBER OF THE NEW SHADOW NETWORK.
THANK YOU, MY KHAN.

I HAVE ASSETS IN PLACE ELSEWHERE, INCLUDING AMONG THE ORGANIZED CRIMINALS KHAN DEPENDS UPON FOR HIS FUNDING.

IVAN BELYAYEV.
RUSSIAN MAFIA.

IVAN WILL DO ANYTHING TO TAKE REVENGE ON KHAN FOR THE DEATH OF HIS SON. AND I'VE GIVEN HIM HIS ORDERS, WHICH HE WILL CARRY OUT....

LEUNG NINH.
VIETNAMESE MAFIA.

...NO MATTER HOW DISTASTEFUL HE MAY FIND THEM.

HOW MUCH LONGER MUST WE ACT THE PART OF ***SHEEP?*** WE ARE THE MOST FEARED MEN IN THE CITY, BUT WHEN KHAN ASKS FOR OUR MONEY, WE TREMBLE AND HAND OVER ALL HE DEMANDS.

DON'T BE A ***FOOL,*** LEUNG.

HE MAKES YOU ***KILL*** YOUR SON WITH YOUR OWN HAND, AND YOU CALL ***ME*** A FOOL FOR WANTING TO RESIST HIM.

YOU HAVE TASTED THE POWER BEHIND HIS THREATS. THERE IS NOTHING THAT WE CAN DO.

YES, RESISTING KHAN COST ME MY SON, BUT THERE ARE OTHERS WHOSE LIVES I VALUE. YOU ALL HAVE THOSE YOU PROTECT, EVEN IF YOUR OWN LIVES MEAN NOTHING TO YOU.

I SAY WE GIVE KHAN WHAT HE ***WANTS.*** AS LONG AS HE IS MAKING MONEY, HE WILL TROUBLE US NO FURTHER.

INTERESTING.

QUEENS. CRANSTON'S LAST REMAINING SAFE HOUSE.
RELAX, MARGO.
THE PIECES ARE MOVING JUST AS I *INTEND*.
YOU SEEM VERY SURE OF YOURSELF.
WITH *GOOD REASON*. THIS IS THE BEST GAME TO PLAY: THE ONE IN WHICH THE ENEMY THINKS HE RUNS THE BOARD.
YEAH, I GET THE *METAPHOR*. THE CONFLICT WITH KHAN IS LIKE A CHESS GAME. ALL VERY 1930s.
I JUST WISH YOU'D INCLUDED SOME 21st CENTURY AMENITIES IN YOUR SAFE HOUSE.
WHAT WOULD HAVING YOUR TECHNOLOGY ADD TO OUR QUALITY OF LIFE. WOULD YOU PREFER WE SPENT THE EVENING *TWITTERING* ONE ANOTHER.
YOU'RE STILL HEALING, SO I'M GOING TO LET THAT SLIDE.

YOU ARE READY FOR TONIGHT? IT'S ABOUT TIME FOR YOU TO GO.
SIGH YOU DON'T HAVE TO *BABY SIT* ME.
CLEARLY NOT.
ARE YOU CHECKING OUT MY ASS?
I'M MERELY DEMONSTRATING MY CONCERN FOR YOUR DERRIÈRE.
I AM QUITE SERIOUS, MARGO. I HOPE YOU WILL BE CAREFUL. HE MAY APPEAR DEFEATED, BUT HE REMAINS A DANGEROUS MAN.
I'M A DANGEROUS WOMAN.
I HAVE NO DOUBT.

БЕЛЫЕФ
HELLO, IVAN. MIND IF I JOIN YOU.
IT IS A TERRIBLE THING WHEN LIFE HAD BEEN SO CRUEL THAT A MAN CANNOT EVEN ENJOY THE COMPANY OF A BEAUTIFUL WOMAN.
I HOPE YOU CAN ENJOY MY COMPANY AT LEAST A LITTLE.
A *LITTLE* ENJOYMENT, THEN. FOR YOU. NOT SINCE MY BELOVED WIFE DIED HAVE I SEEN A WOMAN SO BEAUTIFUL.
I HAVE DONE MANY BAD THINGS IN LIFE. KILLED WITHOUT REMORSE. TORTURED - EVEN *LITTLE CHILDREN*, YES. IS TRUE. BUT BEAUTIFUL WOMAN ALWAYS MAKES PAIN BEARABLE
BUSINESS NOW. PLEASURE LATER *PERHAPS*.

HAVE YOU CONVINCED THE OTHERS TO FOLLOW KHAN?
PERHAPS. MEN IN MY LINE OF WORK ARE OFTEN HAPPY TO EMBRACE *STABILITY*. FOR NOW THEY COOPERATE. TOMORROW, WHO KNOWS?
IT CAUSES FOR ME GREAT ANGUISH, TO ARGUE THAT WE PROP UP KHAN WITH OUR MONIES WHEN I WISH ONLY TO *DESTROY* HIM.
I HOPE YOUR SHADOW KNOWS WHAT HE IS DOING.
THIS IS THE PATH TO *REVENGE*, IVAN. WE ARE PUTTING THE PIECES IN PLACE.
THAT MAKES IT ALL THE EASIER TO KNOCK THEM OVER.
I CAN LIVE WITH COOPERATION AS LONG AS IT IS SET-UP.
OH, ABSOLUTELY. IT IS NOTHING BUT *SET-UP*.

I SAID I'M HERE TO SEE THÔNG.
AND I SAID YOU'RE NOT ON THE LIST.
I WON'T INSULT YOUR LIMITED INTELLIGENCE BY ASKING IF YOU KNOW WHO I AM. YOU KNOW. AND YOU KNOW I'LL HAVE YOUR SISTER RAPED TO DEATH IF YOU DON'T LET ME PASS WITHOUT MAKING A FUSS.
CAN'T ORDER ANYTHING IF YOU'RE DEAD, LEUNG.
CAN'T DO A LOT OF THINGS.
BANG
BANG
BANG
FIND OUT IF THEY HAVE SISTERS, AND IF THEY DO, SEE THEY'RE RAPED TO DEATH. THERE'S A PRINCIPLE HERE.

IF I KNOW THÔNG, HE'LL BE SITTING WITH WHORES, DRINKING TOO MUCH AND, IN GENERAL, MAKING AN IDIOT OF HIMSELF.
I CALLED IT.
KILL A COUPLE OF THE GIRLS TO MAKE A POINT.
I'M GOING TO HATE OWNING THIS PLACE.

AND THAT, LADIES, IS THE SECRET TO FLOURLESS CHOCOLATE CAKE...
WHAT HAPPENED TO THE MUSIC?
HA HA A HA HA HA HA
THÔNG NGUYEN, I HAVE LOOKED INTO YOUR HEART AND SEEN *WEAKNESS* AND *COWARDICE*.
YOUR RIVAL'S MEN ARE HERE TO KILL YOU, AND I SEE *NO REASON* TO STOP THEM.
FLEE, THÔNG NGUYEN, AND CHANGE YOUR LIFE.
THAT WENT BETTER THAN I EXPECTED.
BANG
BANG
UHFFF!

WHAT... WHAT DO YOU WANT FROM ME?
YOU, LEUNG, DESERVE DEATH, BUT I WILL SPARE YOU WHILE YOU *SERVE* THE *SHADOW*.
SERVE? HOW?
YOU SHALL BE THE *ENEMY* OF *MY* ENEMY
SHIWAN KHAN.
OKAY. SURE. YES. WE CAN MAKE A DEAL. I'LL HELP YOU GET KHAN. WORKS FOR ME. WHAT DO YOU NEED ME TO DO?
WE MUST BEGIN WITH HIS ALLIES IN YOUR ORGANIZATION. THERE ARE THOSE WHO WOULD *STRENGTHEN* HIM, AND YOU MUST BEGIN YOUR *ATTACK* THERE.

YOU MEAN...

YES. *IVAN* IS KHAN'S ALLY, AND NOW HE MUST BE YOUR ENEMY.
DESTROY IVAN BELYAYEV.

HE NEXT NIGHT.
HIWAN KHAN'S MANSION.
MAN, THIS PLACE IS AMAZING.
YEAH, I TOTALLY WON THE RELATIVE-FROM-NOWHERE JACKPOT.
THIS IS MY ROOM. I HAVEN'T HAD A CHANCE TO GIVE IT THE PERSONAL TOUCH YET, SO IT'S STILL A LITTLE BIT LIKE A MUSEUM.
YEAH, A TOTALLY COOL MUSEUM.
SO, WHAT DO YOU WANT TO DO NOW, IAN?
HWACK

YOU ABUSE MY GENEROUS NATURE, BATU.
HE WAS HOT!
YOU DO NOT BRING STRANGERS INTO MY HOME. THIS IS NOT A PLACE FOR YOUR DALLIANCES. I DON'T CARE IF YOU WISH TO BE A SLUT, BUT HAVE THE INTELLIGENCE TO BE DISCREET.
SORRY, BUT THIS ISN'T YAK COUNTRY. IN THIS CENTURY, THE DEFINITION OF SLUT IS NOT "NON-VIRGIN."
I DO NOT CARE ABOUT THAT.
I CARE THAT I HAVE CHARGED YOU WITH THE MOST IMPORTANT OF TASKS: TRACKING DOWN AND DESTROYING MY MOST DANGEROUS ENEMY. YOU MUST NOT WASTE YOUR TIME WITH FOOLISHNESS.
I CAN DO BOTH, YOU KNOW. I'M ON THE SHADOW. BUT A GIRL'S GOT TO HAVE HER FUN.
NOT UNTIL YOU COMPLETE YOUR TASKS AND PROVE YOURSELF. DISPOSE OF THE BODY.
SOMEONE'S GOT ISSUES.
HE KILLS MY HOTTIE, AND I HAVE T DISPOSE OF THE BOD WHAT AN ASSHOLE.

DON'T YOU GET ALL MONGOLIAN SCARY ON ME. I *INVENTED* THAT SHIT.
WELL, I GUESS YOU DID FIRST, BUT I INVENTED IT ON MY OWN WITHOUT KNOWING YOU INVENTED IT FIRST.
I HAD HOPED YOU WOULD BE *MATURE* ENOUGH TO REQUIRE NO PARENTING.
THAT'S WHAT YOU CALL STABBING A POTENTIAL BOYFRIEND IN THE BACK?
YOU DID TAKE THE DAGGER OUT BEFORE BURNING HIM, YES?
M NOT A MORON.
ON THAT WE AGREE, WHICH IS WHY I EXPECT MUCH OF YOU. I NEED TO BE ABLE TO DEPEND UPON YOU WITHOUT SUPERVISION.
IN YOU I HAVE RECRUITED AN ASSOCIATE AND POTENTIAL *HEIR,* NOT, I HOPE, A BURDEN.
BELIEVE ME, I APPRECIATE THE TRUST, AND I WON'T LET YOU DOWN. AND YOU DON'T WANT ME TO BRING BOYS HERE--I GET IT. I JUST WISHED YOU'D MENTIONED IT BEFORE KILLING HIM.
BUT YOU UNDERSTAND MY ACTIONS.
YEAH, I GET YOU.
BUT I AM T GOING TO RGET THIS, GRAMPS.
AS FOR THE SHADOW, I'M PUTTING THINGS IN MOTION. *TONIGHT*.
PORKY, YOU READY TO MAKE SOME MONEY?

BATU, GIRL. I'M ALWAYS READY.
MONROE AND HIS BOYS HAVE BEEN GIVING US TROUBLE FOR YEARS.
HELLS YEAH. THEY ARE SOME SCARY MOTHERS.
THEY GET IN A FIGHT, THEY DON'T CARE IF THEY LIVE OR DIE, AND THEY DON'T CARE WHO THEY MESS UP. THEY GOT MORE AND BIGGER GUNS THAN WE'LL EVER HAVE, WHICH IS WHY WE NEVER TOOK THEM ON.
NOW WE GET RID OF TWO BIRDS WITH ONE STONE. I SEND THE SHADOW HIS DISTRESS CODE, AND SEND HIM KICKING ASS INTO THAT BUILDING.
IF HE SURVIVES, THEN ONCE HE'S DONE CLEANING UP OUR MESS, WE CLEAN HIM UP.
THEN WE GET PAID.

MARGO RECEIVED A MESSAGE FROM THE GANG MEMBER, PORKY. HE SAYS HE IS PINNED DOWN BY A TWISTED GANG OF CRIMINALS LED BY A MAN KNOWN ONLY AS MONROE.
DRUG PEDDLERS, MURDERERS, ARSONISTS. THEY'RE HUMAN *GARBAGE*. THEIR LIVES HAVE NO MEANING.
LET'S SEE ABOUT THEIR *DEATHS*.
BANG BANG
BANG BANG
LET'S ADD *KIDNAPPING* AND *SERIAL RAPE* TO THE LIST. WOMEN HAVE BEEN *DISAPPEARING* IN THIS PART OF BROOKLYN. MYSTERY *SOLVED*.
NO TIME FOR *THEATRICS*. MAYBE SOMEONE GAVE THESE MEN A CHANCE LONG AGO. MAYBE THEY NEVER HAD A CHANCE.
THEY'RE NOT GETTING
DEAD, MAYBE A FEW HOURS. ALWAYS GOOD TO KNOW THE BAD GUYS HAD IT COMING.

YOU GOT THEM.
THEY WERE HERE LIKE YOU SAID. YOU, HOWEVER, WERE *NOT*.
IMPORTANT THING IS THEY'RE DEAD.
WISH I COULD KILL THEM AGAIN.
YOU KNOW WHAT? PRETTY SOON I'LL BE SAYING THAT ABOUT *YOU*.
BANG
BANG
BANG
BANG
BANG
BANG

AIM FOR THE CEILING. THAT THING IS ABOUT TO COME DOWN, SO MIGHT AS WELL BRING IT DOWN ON HIM.
CRASH
UGH...
LET'S SEE WHAT THIS FOOL LOOKS LIKE.
SWEET.

SSSSSSSSSSSSSSSSS

ATER THAT
IGHT.
WE HAD HIM. I SWEAR WE DID. BUT THEN THE TEAR GAS CANISTER CAME IN, AND WE HAD TO BEAT. NOTHING ELSE WE COULD HAVE DONE.
PERHAPS NOT.
I THOUGHT YOU WERE GOING TO BE MAD. YOU DON'T LOOK MAD.
I'M NOT. NOT AT ALL.
YOU AND YOUR GANG CAME SO CLOSE. ANOTHER FEW SECONDS WOULD HAVE MADE THE DIFFERENCE. I'M NOT ANGRY. I'M PSYCHED!
YOU WERE UNLUCKY, BUT THE SHADOW WAS CARELESS AND SLOPPY AND INEPT. HE'S CLEARLY NOT THE BAD ASS HE USED TO BE, AND THAT MEANS THIS JOB IS TOTALLY DOABLE.
SO WE GET ANOTHER CHANCE?
NO, YOU'RE BURNED.
BANG
WHICH IS TOO BAD, REALLY. COMING UP WITH ANOTHER APPROACH WILL BE TRICKY.
BUT NOT IMPOSSIBLE.
SURE THINGS COULD HAVE GONE BETTER, BUT I'M STILL READY TO CALL THIS A PRETTY GOOD NIGHT.

CLINK
I'D SAY THIS HAS BEEN A VERY GOOD NIGHT.
WORTH THE RISK OF DINING OUT IN PUBLIC.
NO ONE WILL NOTICE US. AND I'D SAY WE'VE EARNED A LITTLE CELEBRATING. YOU WERE WONDERFUL, MARGO.
I JUST HAD TO TOSS IN A CANISTER OF TEAR GAS ON CUE. YOU HAD TO LET A BUILDING COLLAPSE ON YOU.
AND YOU HAD TO PRETEND TO BE HELPLESS, WHICH I KNOW IS HARD FOR YOUR OLD-TIMEY IDEAS ABOUT MASCULINITY.
IN REAL LIFE, STRATEGY CAN BE A BIT TRICKIER THAN ON THE CHESS BOARD. BUT THE EFFORT IS WORTHWHILE. THE PIECES ARE ALL IN PLACE.
AND NOW?
THE ENEMY SUSPECTS WE ARE WEAK, SO I'D SAY OUR MOVE IS OBVIOUS.
WE PRESS THE ADVANTAGE.

ISSUE #5 COVER

WORLEY

ITTLE ODESSA.
IT'S ONE OF HIS BIGGEST MONEY-MAKERS.
CREDIT CARDS.
IVAN RUNS THE WHOLE SHOW FROM RIGHT HERE.
LEUNG NINH. VIETNAMESE MAFIA.
HACKING INTO ACCOUNTS TO STEAL NUMBERS, THEN USING THEM TO BUY GIFT CARDS, WHICH HE SELLS ONLINE AT A DISCOUNT.
NICE SET UP.
I KNOW THE SHADOW WANTS YOU MESSING WITH IVAN, BUT YOU SURE THIS IS A GOOD IDEA? WAY I SEE IT, THE SHADOW TARGETS MEN WHO DO WHAT WE'RE ABOUT TO DO.
HE TARGETS CRIMINALS. IVAN HAS AT LEAST ONE HUNDRED COMPUTERS, TWO HUNDRED WORKERS, INCLUDING WOMEN AND CHILDREN.
ALL OF THEM CRIMINALS.
WHEN THE SHADOW ASKED ME TO TAKE OUT IVAN, HE DIDN'T SAY THERE COULDN'T BE COLLATERAL DAMAGE.

ANYHOW, WORD ON THE STREET IS THAT THE SHADOW IS OLD, HUNTING DOWN MUGGERS AND HELPING OLD LADIES CROSS THE STREET.
HE THINKS HE'S USING ME, BUT I'M USING HIM.
BUT YOU'RE STILL HESITATING.
I'M NOT HESITATING.
I AM SAVORING.
IVAN SHOULDN'T HAVE CROSSED ME. HE SHOULDN'T HAVE TRIED TO HUMILIATE ME.
THOSE WOMEN AND CHILDREN, THEY PAY THE PRICE FOR HIS MISTAKES.
BOOOM
AND IVAN, ONCE MORE, LOSES WHAT HE CARES ABOUT MOST.

EVERYONE WAS EVACUATED HOURS AGO. I APPRECIATE THE WARNING, MARGO.
AS LONG AS YOU FOLLOW THE SHADOW'S INSTRUCTIONS, WE'LL TAKE CARE OF YOU.
I AM NOT DOING THIS FOR THE SHADOW.
HE KNOWS. JUST SO LONG AS YOU DO IT.
IVAN BELYAYEV. RUSSIAN MAFIA.
IF YOU WILL EXCUSE ME, DEAR LADY, I HAVE BUSINESS TO TEND TO.
BLAM BLAM
BLAM BLAM
GET ME OUT OF HERE!

IVAN KNEW WE WERE COMING.
KIND OF MAKES YOU WONDER, DOESN'T IT?
WONDER WHAT?
CHINATOWN.
"IF HE KNEW WE WERE COMING, THEN WHAT ELSE DOES HE HAVE PLANNED."
BOOM
BOOM
BOOM

NO CIVILIANS WERE HURT. I MADE SURE EVERYONE WAS WARNED. BUT WE'RE NOT GOING TO BE ABLE TO *CONTAIN* THIS FOR LONG.
THEY'RE GOING TO FIGURE OUT WE'VE BEEN PLAYING THEM BOTH AGAINST EACH OTHER. YOU'RE NOT READY TO FACE BOTH KHAN AND THOSE CRIME LORDS.
I DON'T THINK IVAN AND LEUNG ARE GOING TO START COMPARING NOTES.
YOU'RE NOT SEEING THE BIG PICTURE.
THEY'LL READ THE PAPERS OR WATCH THE NEWS.
IF THEY FIGURE OUT NO ONE'S ACTUALLY BEEN HURT ON EITHER SIDE, WE'RE IN TROUBLE.
TRUST ME. I CAN HANDLE THE BIG PICTURE.
THERE WON'T BE TIME FOR IVAN AND LEUNG TO COMPARE NOTES.
I HOPE YOU'RE RIGHT. I'M BETTING MY LIFE THAT YOU ARE.
IT'S A SAFE BET. BUT YOU OUGHT TO BRACE YOURSELF.
THINGS ARE ABOUT TO GET VERY *INTERESTING.*

MIDTOWN HEADQUARTERS. SHIWAN KHAN'S OPERATION.
EXCUSE ME, MY KHAN. I HAVE SOME NEWS.
THERE WAS AN INCIDENT INVOLVING TWO OF YOUR, *UH,* FINANCIAL SOURCES.
IVAN BELYAYEV AND LEUNG NINH.
THEY SEEM TO HAVE LAUNCHED ***ASSAULTS*** AT ONE ANOTHER. A NUMBER OF BUILDINGS APPEAR TO HAVE EXPLODED.
PEARL
YOU WERE MEANT TO MAKE SURE NOTHING LIKE THIS HAPPENED.
KRAK
I ADVISE YOU ALL TO DO YOUR JOBS.

to: Margo
Having desired effect
RICK ROSE,
ADOW AGENT.
KRASH
TEXT YOUR WIFE ON YOUR OWN TIME. I NEED THAT REFINED LIST OF POSSIBLE RELAY STATIONS.
BEFORE MORNING, MY KHAN. YOU WILL HAVE YOUR CHOICE OF STATIONS, AND YOU WILL HAVE ALL THE POWER YOU NEED.

CHECK IT OUT, PEOPLE. I JUST ORDERED DONUTS AND COFFEE. THEY'LL BE HERE IN FIVE MINUTES, SO TAKE A BREAK.
AND SOMEONE CALL LIKE AN AMBULANCE OR A HEARSE OR WHATEVER FOR THAT GUY.
HEY!
MUST YOU PLAY THE CLOWN?
I'M TRYING TO KEEP THINGS UNDER CONTROL. PEOPLE WON'T WORK IF THEY'RE AFRAID THAT EVERY TIME YOU DON'T LIKE SOMETHING YOU'RE GOING TO, LIKE, CRUSH THEIR JAWS.
I AM TRYING TO UNDO THE DAMAGE THAT YEARS OF PRISON HAVE DONE TO MY BODY. I NEED POWER TO USE MY REGENERATION DEVICE.
I DON'T NEED LESSONS IN MANAGEMENT FROM A CHILD--PARTICULARLY ONE WHO HAS FAILED AT HER TASKS.
IF YOU HAD STOPPED THE SHADOW LIKE I COMMANDED YOU--
THE SHADOW. GIVE ME A BREAK. THAT GUY IS A JOKE, NOT THE BOGEYMAN YOU THINK HE IS. I'M NOT GOING TO TAKE THE BLAME FOR YOUR MESSES.

LATER THAT NIGHT.
HE NEEDS MASSIVE AMOUNTS OF POWER. I DON'T REALLY UNDERSTAND WHY.
SOME KIND OF EXPERIMENT HAVING TO DO WITH HIS AGING, BUT THAT'S AS MUCH AS HE'S LET SLIP.
THE HYPNOSIS TECHNIQUES YOU TAUGHT ME SEEM TO BE WORKING. HE DOESN'T SUSPECT ME.
I'LL TRY TO FIND OUT MORE, BUT THE BOTTOM LINE IS THAT HE'S GOING TO USE ONE OF THESE RELAY STATIONS TO REROUTE VIRTUALLY ALL OF THE CITY'S POWER FOR HIMSELF.
WHY HE IS DOING IT DOESN'T MATTER. STOPPING IT DOES. THE CONSEQUENCES OF A CITY-WIDE BLACKOUT WOULD BE CATASTROPHIC.
WHAT ABOUT KHAN'S MEETING WITH THE CRIME BOSSES? IS THAT GOING TO HAPPEN?
TOMORROW. JUST LIKE YOU PREDICTED.
IF WE SUFFICIENTLY INTERRUPT HIS CASH FLOW, THAT WILL DIVERT HIS ATTENTION, MAYBE EVEN SHUT HIM DOWN. BUT IS IVAN GOING TO BE ABLE TO HANDLE KHAN?
I'VE DONE WHAT I CAN DO FOR HIM.
I HOPE THAT'S ENOUGH.
IVAN IS READY.

ONE WEEK EARLIER.
"YOU TEACH ME YOUR SECRETS. I AM HONORED."
OGUUHA
AND IF KHAN WISHES TO FORCE MY HAND, AS HE DID WHEN HE FORCED ME TO KILL MY OWN SON...THIS WILL PROTECT ME?
NO.
I CANNOT SHOW YOU HOW TO RESIST HIS WILL. TRAINING OF THAT SORT WOULD TAKE YEARS.
BUT I CAN TEACH YOU SOME TECHNIQUES TO KEEP HIM FROM SENSING YOUR INTENTIONS.
BUT YOU MUST KNOW WHAT YOU ARE AGREEING TO. YOUR CHANCES OF SURVIVING ARE NOT STRONG.
IT IS WHAT I WISH.
BUT YOU SEEM NOT SO WORRIED ABOUT MY SURVIVAL.
YOU WANT REVENGE, AND SO YOU AGREE TO BE MY TOOL. I WILL HAPPILY USE YOU. BUT YOU, IVAN BELYAYEV, ARE GUILTY OF MURDER, EXTORTION, TORTURE AND HUMAN TRAFFICKING.
I WON'T TROUBLE MYSELF TO TALK YOU INTO PRESERVING YOURSELF.
I LIKE YOUR COLD FATALISM. YOU WOULD HAVE MADE A GOOD RUSSIAN.

TODAY.
SECURE THE PERIMETER. I WANT NO ONE COMING IN OR OUT DURING THE MEETING.
YES, MY KHAN.
YOU GUYS JUST COULDN'T KEEP YOUR CRAP UNDER CONTROL. NOW WE'RE ALL CALLED IN TO THE PRINCIPAL'S OFFICE.
CHRIST. I'VE GOT THINGS TO DO, BUT I HAVE TO SIT HERE AND WATCH YOU TWO GET MONGOLIAN *BARBECUED.*
KILL HIM.
BLAM
IS THERE ANYONE ELSE WHO WISHES TO BE EXCUSED FROM HEARING WHAT I HAVE TO SAY?
THEN WE MAY BEGIN.

YOU TWO, WITH YOUR FEUD, HAVE COST ME MONEY.
I WILL ACCEPT NO MORE DISRUPTIONS IN MY CASH FLOW.
YOU BOTH CONTROL POWERFUL INTERESTS. IF YOU DO NOT WISH TO SEE THEM PROSPER, I AM SURE YOU HAVE SUBORDINATES WHO WILL PROVE BETTER STEWARDS.
I AM A REASONABLE MAN, AND I UNDERSTAND DISAGREEMENTS CAN ARISE. ANY OUTSTANDING COMPLAINTS MUST BE ADDRESSED NOW. AFTER THIS MEETING, FAILURE TO COMPLY WITH MY WISHES WILL RESULT IN YOUR *REMOVAL.*
DO EITHER OF YOU WISH TO SPEAK ON THIS SUBJECT?
FORGIVE ME, MY KHAN. I ALLOWED MY *PASSIONS* TO COMMAND MY JUDGMENT.

BLAM BLAM BLAM BLAM BLAM BLAM

BLAM BLAM BLAM BLAM

BLAM

HOW COULD YOU HAVE HOPED TO KILL ME WITH SO SLOPPY AN ATTACK?

I DID NOT MEAN TO KILL YOU WITH MY GUN.

BUT WITH MY *BOMB.*

WE WERE LUCKY HE MEANT ONLY TO DESTROY THE ROOM.
AND EVERYONE IN IT.
ALL OF THE HEADS OF THE FAMILIES ARE DEAD. THEIR EMPIRES WILL BE IN CHAOS.
AND IVAN WAS ABLE TO DETONATE THE DEVICE WITHOUT MY SENSING HIS INTENTIONS.
SOMEONE MUST HAVE TAUGHT HIM HOW TO SHIELD HIS THOUGHTS FROM MINE.
THE SHADOW REMAINS A PROBLEM. AND A THREAT.

"ALLOWING ANOTHER MAN TO ASSAULT ME IS NOT HIS WAY, SO WHY WOULD HE REVEAL HIS HAND IF HE DID NOT HAVE SOMETHING BIGGER IN MIND?"
THERE WAS AN *ATTEMPT* ON THE KHAN'S LIFE. EVERYTHING IS BEING SPED UP.
THERE IT IS.
WHAT ARE YOU DOING WITH MY FILES, DERICK?

THIS IS UNACCEPTABLE.
I CHARGED YOU WITH REMOVING HIM FROM THE EQUATION.
AND I AM WORKING ON THAT, BUT THIS ATTACK WASN'T THE SHADOW. TRUST ME. HE'S WASHED UP. THE GUY COULD BARELY ESCAPE FROM A BUNCH OF THIRD-RATE GANG BANGERS.
BUT HE DID ESCAPE.
BECAUSE HE GOT LUCKY.
IF YOU THINK THIS SABOTAGE OF ONE OF OUR PRINCIPAL SOURCES OF INCOME IS NOT THE SHADOW'S WORK, THEN YOU DO NOT UNDERSTAND THE ENEMY.
I UNDERSTAND YOU'RE, LIKE, OBSESSED WITH THE GUY.
I UNDERSTAND THE SHADOW WAS A PAIN IN YOUR ASS BACK WHEN MOVIE THEATERS HAD THEIR OWN PIANO PLAYERS, BUT THIS IS TODAY. HE'S LIKE A MILLION YEARS OLD NOW, AND YOU ARE LIVING IN THE PAST.

KRAK

YOU ARE AN ARROGANT CHILD WHO KNOWS NOTHING. I GAVE YOU TOO MUCH AUTHORITY BECAUSE I WAS BLINDED BY MY DESIRE FOR FAMILY.
DO YOU REALLY WANT TO GET ON MY CASE BECAUSE I HAVEN'T BEEN ABLE TO DO THE ONE THING YOU'VE TRIED TO DO OVER AND OVER AGAIN YOUR WHOLE LIFE AND ALWAYS FAILED AT?

YOU KNOW WHAT? I AM SICK OF YOUR PATRIARCHAL CRAP. I AM OUT OF HERE.
YOU WOULD DARE ABANDON YOUR DUTY?

NO, I PLAN TO FULFILL MY DUTY.
I JUST DON'T WANT MY ANNOYING FAMILY BREATHING DOWN MY NECK WHILE I DO IT.

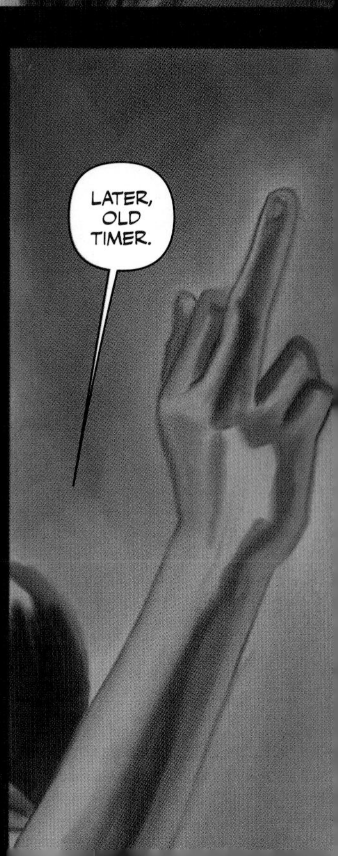
LATER, OLD TIMER.

ONE HOUR LATER.
"I HAVE NO CHOICE. I MUST BEGIN NOW."
MY ENEMIES HAVE BEEN DOGGING MY HEELS. I CANNOT LET THEM GET AHEAD OF ME. WE MUST BEGIN THE PROCEDURE AT ONCE.
INFORM OUR MEN AT THE RELAY STATION THAT THEY MUST BEGIN TO DIVERT POWER IMMEDIATELY. I WILL THEN REQUIRE ONE HOUR BEFORE I CAN USE THE REJUVENATION DEVICE.
I SHALL GO THERE NOW, BUT REMAIN IN CONTACT VIA THE INTERCOM.
YES, MY KHAN. BUT WHAT OF THE PRISONER.
"SHOULD WE INTERROGATE THIS DERICK ROSE?"
HE WILL KNOW NOTHING OF VALUE. *KILL* HIM.

HAS THE RELAY STATION BEEN ACTIVATED?
YES, MY KHAN.
WHEN THE POWER GOES DOWN, OUR BUILDING WILL BE THE ONLY STRUCTURE IN THE CITY STILL ILLUMINATED. THAT WILL ATTRACT THE AUTHORITIES, WHO MAY INVESTIGATE BEFORE THE HOUR HAS PASSED.
KEEP THEM OUT, AT THE COST OF YOUR LIVES IF YOU MUST.
YES, MY KHAN.
GIVE THE WORD TO COMMENCE THE PROCEDURE.
PLUNGE THE CITY INTO *DARKNESS.*

DERICK NEVER ARRIVED AT THE MEET. I HAVE TO ASSUME HE'S BEEN FOUND OUT.
THEY'LL LIKELY *KILL* HIM.
NOT IF I GET TO HIM FIRST.
IT WILL BE *CHAOS* OUT THERE.
IT WILL BE *DARK.*
KHAN HAS PLUNGED THE CITY INTO SHADOW. THE *ADVANTAGE* IS *MINE.*

IX HOURS AGO.
ITTLE ODESSA.
IVAN IS GONE. MANY OF OUR FRIENDS ARE DEAD. OUR MOST SEASONED LEADERS HAVE BEEN LOST. BUT WE MUST CARRY ON.
THOSE VIETNAMESE ЖОПЫ DROVE IVAN TO WHAT HE DID, AND THEY'LL PAY, BUT WE NEED TO TAKE CARE OF BUSINESS FIRST.
ONE OF THIS WOULD HAVE APPENED IF KHAN HAD NOT BEEN BLEEDING US DRY.
HE PUSHED IVAN TO THE EDGE.
WE FINISH KHAN, THEN WE TAKE CARE OF THE VIETNAMESE.
THEN WE OWN THIS TOWN.
YES!
WE KILL HIM.
AGREED!
THERE IS NO MORE DELAY. WE MOVE TONIGHT.
I HAVE OBEYED YOUR COMMANDS, SHADOW. WE WILL STRIKE AS YOU WISH.
GOOD. YOU WILL REMEMBER NONE OF THIS, ONLY THAT IT IS YOUR OWN IDEA TO TAKE KHAN DOWN.

FOUR HOURS AGO.
CHINATOWN.
THE RUSSIANS KILLED OUR BEST MINDS, OUR BRAVEST WARRIORS. THEY WILL PAY FOR WHAT THEY'VE DONE. I PROMISE YOU THEY WILL BLEED, BUT THAT CAN WAIT FOR TOMORROW.
REMOVING THE RUSSIANS WON'T GET US ANYTHING IF THE SPOILS OF WAR ARE STOLEN FROM US.
THEY KILLED LEUNG. ONE MORE DAY WITHOUT REVENGE IS TOO LONG.
I UNDERSTAND YOUR ANGER, BUT WE MUST DO MORE THAN HURT THE RUSSIANS. WE MUST BE IN A POSITION TO TAKE WHAT IS THEIRS.
KHAN WILL DIE TONIGHT, AND WHEN HE'S GONE, WE CAN UNLEASH OUR FULL VENOM ON THE RUSSIANS.
I UNDERSTAND. WE WILL DO IT YOUR WAY, AND WE WILL MAKE THOSE RUSSIANS PAY.
NOW IF YOU GENTLEMEN WILL EXCUSE ME.
I MUST MAKE THE FINAL PREPARATIONS FOR TONIGHT'S ASSAULT.

NOW.

THE *PIECES* HAVE BEEN SET. THE *PLAYERS* ARE IN MOTION, AND THE *STAKES* ARE DANGEROUSLY HIGH.

KHAN HAS SIPHONED OFF THE POWER THROUGHOUT THE CITY. I STILL DON'T KNOW WHAT ITS PURPOSE IS, BUT I BELIEVE HE HOPES THAT THE CITY WILL DESCEND INTO CHAOS.

THAT MAY NOT BE HIS PRIMARY GOAL, BUT HE KNOWS IT WILL KEEP POLICE TOO BUSY TO FIND HIM.

I'M ALMOST THERE, MARGO.

HOW DO THE STREETS LOOK?

TENSE.

MAYBE YOU FELLAS SHOULD MOVE ALONG.

WHAT, CAUSE THE LIGHTS GO OUT, WE CAN'T STAND ON THE SIDEWALK.

STREETS FULL OF PEOPLE. HOW COME YOU'RE ONLY BOTHERING US?

NOW, LET'S KEEP OUR TEMPERS.

MILLIONS OF PEOPLE, NO POWER, AND LIMITED LAW ENFORCEMENT. IT'S ONLY A MATTER OF TIME BEFORE THE BODIES START PILING UP.

I'M KEEPING THE LINE OPEN. WHEN I GET THE INFORMATION, YOU'LL KNOW WHAT TO DO.

I'M STANDING BY.

IN THE MEANTIME, YOUR EVAC IS READY.

I NEED TO FIND MY CAPTURED AGENT AND DETERMINE JUST WHAT THE HELL KHAN IS DOING. BECAUSE WHATEVER IT IS...

"...I HAVE A FEELING IT IS GOING TO BE VERY, VERY BAD."

CON EDISON PLANT.
ASTORIA, QUEENS.
NO ONE KNOWS WE'RE HERE, RIGHT?
BY THE TIME THEY FIGURE OUT WHERE WE ARE, WE'LL BE GONE. KHAN NEEDS ANOTHER HOUR AT THE MOST.
IN ALL THIS CHAOS, IT WILL BE AT LEAST TWICE AS LONG BEFORE ANYONE REALIZES THERE'S SOMETHING WRONG HERE.
SO WHAT'S WITH ALL THE MUSCLE AND FIREPOWER.
CLICK
BECAUSE YOU CAN'T BE TOO CAREFUL. AND MAYBE, JUST MAYBE, WE'LL GET *LUCKY*....
...AND THE *SHADOW* WILL FIGURE OUT WHERE WE ARE.
YOU *WANT* HIM HERE?
MY GRANDFATHER THINKS I CAN'T TAKE OUT THAT OLD FOSSIL. IF THE SHADOW SHOWS UP, I'M GONG TO PROVE I CAN DO WHAT THE MIGHTY SHIWAN KHAN NEVER COULD.

KHAN'S MIDTOWN HEADQUARTERS.

MOSTLY DESERTED. ALL THE ACTIVITY SEEMS TO BE ON THE UPPER FLOORS.

WIDE ANGLE, NO AVOIDING IT.

CRACK

THEY'LL THINK THE CAMERA IS DOWN.

OR THEY'LL SUSPECT THEY HAVE AN *INTRUDER*.

BANG

BUT IT WAS ONLY A MATTER OF TIME BEFORE THEY FIGURED THAT OUT.

BANG BANG BANG
MIGHT AS WELL MAKE IT WORK FOR ME.
WE'VE GOT A CAMERA OUT TWO FLOORS DOWN.
COULD BE A SHORT IN THE--
BANG BANG BANG
I DON'T GIVE A CRAP WHAT YOU'RE DOING. YOU NEED TO GET A TEAM TWO FLOORS DOWN. THERE'S GUNFIRE.
DO YOU UNDERSTAND THAT HE HAS BEGUN THE PROCESS. AND WE'VE GOT AN INTRUDER. MOVE!
OR KHAN WILL KILL US ALL.

YOU'RE TOUGHER THAN YOU LOOK, DERRICK, I'LL GIVE YOU THAT. I GUESS YOU WERE HOLDING OUT UNTIL YOU WERE RESCUED OR UNTIL WE LOST PATIENCE AND KILLED YOU.
CONGRATULATIONS. ONE OF THOSE THINGS IS NOW HAPPENING. TOO BAD. I'D HAVE LIKED TO HAVE BROKEN YOU.
IT WAS THE SHADOW'S TRAINING. THAT'S WHAT TAUGHT ME HOW TO HOLD OUT. TAUGHT ME SOMETHING ELSE TOO.
YEAH, WHAT'S THAT?
THAT WAITING TO BE RESCUED ISN'T SUCH A BAD IDEA.
KRAK

I NEED TO KNOW WHAT KHAN'S UP TO.

I DON'T THINK WE HAVE A LOT OF TIME. GUARDS HAVE BEEN ROTATING IN AND OUT PRETTY REGULARLY.

I THINK THEY'RE GOING TO HAVE OTHER THINGS TO WORRY ABOUT. NOW, TELL ME WHAT YOU KNOW.

I STILL HAVEN'T FIGURED OUT WHAT THE HELL KHAN NEEDS THE POWER FOR, BUT WHATEVER IT IS, HE'S DRAWING THROUGH A RELAY AT THE CON ED PLANT IN ASTORIA.

THEN THAT'S WHERE WE GO.

COME ON. THE ROOM WE NEED IS A FEW DOORS DOWN.

IN HERE.

CRASH

WHY THE HELL ARE WE GOING THAT WAY? THERE'S A STAIRWELL.

CAN'T USE IT. SO I'VE ARRANGED *ALTERNATE* TRANSPORTATION.

DON'T GET ME WRONG. A WINDOW WASHER'S PLATFORM IS ANYONE'S IDEA OF A SWEET RIDE. BUT ***WHY*** ARE WE ESCAPING? DON'T YOU WANT TO STOP KHAN FROM DOING WHATEVER THE HELL HE'S GONE TO SO MUCH TROUBLE TO DO?

NUMBER ONE, GETTING THE POWER BACK ON NEEDS TO BE OUR FIRST PRIORITY. NUMBER TWO, WHEN WE SHUT OFF THE POWER, WE STOP KHAN AT THE SAME TIME.

"AND NUMBER THREE HAS A WHOLE LOT TO DO WITH WHY WE CAN'T USE THE STAIRWELL."
BANG
BANG
HA! GOT ONE.
I HAVE BEEN GIVEN INFORMATION. WE GO THIS WAY.
IT IS TIME TO AVENGE OUR RUSSIAN BROTHERS.
BANG
BANG BANG
BANG
KHAN, YOUR MEN DIE FOR YOU! ARE YOU TOO MUCH COWARD TO FACE US?
КАКОГО ЧЕРТА!

IT'S OUR LUCKY DAY! WE GET TO KILL BOTH OUR ENEMIES AT ONCE!
địt cái lổn mẹ m!
BANG
BANG
BANG
BANG
BANG
IT'S A FREAKING CIRCLE JERK. HOW IN THE HELL DID THEY BOTH SHOW UP AT THE EXACT SAME TIME.
WE'VE ALL BEEN *PLAYED!*

THE TIMING HAD TO BE *PERFECT*. IT WAS.
SO, YOU *ELIMINATE* KHAN'S MEN ALONG WITH TWO CRIME FAMILIES. NICE.
I'M NOT SURE THEY WILL ALL BE ELIMINATED, BUT AT THE VERY LEAST THEY'LL KEEP KHAN'S MEN BUSY UNTIL WE CAN GET THE POWER BACK ON.
THEN LET'S TAKE CARE OF IT.
OFFICER, BY SERVING ME, YOU SERVE THE CITY. ARE YOU READY TO OBEY.
YES.
DERRICK, YOU'VE DONE AMAZING WORK AS MY AGENT. THINGS ARE GOING TO GET DANGEROUS, BUT I *NEED* YOU FOR THIS.
UNDERSTOOD. I'M READY TO SEE IT THROUGH.
ARE YOU TRYING TO GET ME TO RIDE IN THE BACK?
SORRY. THIS BLACK MAN DOES NOT GET IN THE BACK OF A POLICE CAR.

SHOULD I CALL FOR BACKUP.
DERRICK, WAIT FOR MY SIGNAL.
YES. AND *AMBULANCES*.
YOU HEAR THAT?
YEAH, LIKE RATS OR SOMETHING.
I THOUGHT I HEARD SOMEONE COCKING A PISTOL.
RATS DON'T CARRY PISTOLS, MORON.
CLICK
BANG BANG
BANG BANG

BANG BANG BANG
LET'S GET READY.
HA HA HA HA HA HA HA!
THIS IS WHERE IT ENDS. THIS IS WHERE YOUR EVIL FINDS ITS JUST REWARD.
ENOUGH BRAGGING, SHADOW. YOU CAN HIDE ALL NIGHT, OR YOU CAN STEP UP AND ACT LIKE A MAN.
BANG BANG
BANG
HA HA HA HA HA HA HA HA!

COME OUT, YOUNG LADY. IT IS NOT TOO LATE TO TURN YOUR BACK ON YOUR EVIL DEEDS.
LOVE IT. IT'S LIKE AN OLD WEST DUEL OR SOMETHING. WE'LL SEE WHICH OF US IS QUICKER ON THE DRAW.
NO, WE WON'T.
BANG
WAS THAT REALLY NECESSARY.
DON'T BE SUCH A SEXIST. YOU SHOOT MEN WITHOUT THINKING TWICE.
THIS IS WHAT THE MODERN ERA IS LIKE. EQUAL OPPORTUNITY.
IT'S CLEAR, DERRICK. LET'S MOVE. CLOCK'S TICKING.

ME SEE WHAT WE'VE GOT.
OKAY, THIS DOESN'T SEEM TOO HARD.
ALL I HAVE TO DO IS...WHAT?
ZING
I NEED FIVE MINUTES, TOPS. KEEP THEM OFF OF ME.
SHE'S GONE. MUST HAVE BEEN WEARING A VEST UNDER THAT JACKET...
SHE WON'T GET FAR.
NO, I'LL TRACK DOWN THE GIRL.
DAMN IT, MARGO. I KNOW YOU AREN'T IMPRESSED BY MY REPUTATION, BUT--
ARE YOU KIDDING ME? AFTER EVERYTHING I'VE SEEN YOU DO? BUT KEEPING DERRICK WORKING IS OUR PRIORITY.
AND KICKING THIS TEENAGER'S ASS WILL BE MY PLEASURE.

BANG
BANG
WHY ARE YOU EVEN DOING THIS? SHOULDN'T YOU BE AT A CHEERLEADING CLINIC OR SOMETHING?
CHEAP SHOT, FIRING AT ME FROM BEHIND.
GIRLIE, I'M JUST GETTING STARTED.
I'M DOING IT BECAUSE MY ASSHOLE GRANDFATHER THINKS I *CAN'T*.
THAT'S YOUR MOTIVATION FOR MASS MURDER?
BANG
YOU DON'T KNOW WHAT THE HELL YOU'RE TALKING ABOUT. I HAD *NOTHING*, AND THEN MY GRANDFATHER FOUND ME.
AND THAT WAS EVEN *WORSE*.
NOW I'M GOING TO BEAT HIM AT HIS OWN GAME. I'M GOING TO *KILL* THE *SHADOW*.

BANG
POINT BLANK SHOT AT SOMEONE WHO ISN'T LOOKING IS ONE THING. HITTING A MOVING TARGET IS ANOTHER.
YOU'RE NOT CUT OUT FOR THIS.
I'M SMARTER, FASTER, AND I'VE GOT MOVES YOU CAN'T SEE COMING.
BANG BANG BANG
I SAW THAT ONE COMING.
ZZZZZZZZZZZZZZZZZZZZZZZ
AND MISSION ACCOMPLISHED.

POWER'S BACK.
THE LIGHTS COMING ON WERE A DEAD GIVEAWAY.
THAT WAS KIND OF EXCESSIVE, DON'T YOU THINK.
SHE'S WEARING A VEST, SO WHAT THE HELL. SHE GOT UP LAST TIME. I'M JUST MAKING SURE.
BANG
BANG
SHE MADE ME MAD.
YEAH, I PICKED UP ON THAT.
COPS WILL BE ON THE WAY. THEY'LL TAKE HER TO A *HOSPITAL* OR A *MORGUE*, WHICHEVER SUITS BEST.
AND KHAN?
WE WOULD NEVER GET THERE IN TIME TO TAKE ACTION. THE COPS WILL BE SWARMING THAT BUILDING NOW THAT THE POWER'S BACK.

"I HAVE A FEELING THEY'RE GOING TO FIND A BLOODBATH."

JESUS CHRIST. YOU EVER SEE ANYTHING LIKE THIS. GONNA BE A LOT OF ***OVERTIME*** TONIGHT.

ENJOY IT. LOOKS LIKE HALF THE BAD GUYS IN THE CITY BOUGHT IT IN HERE. THINGS ARE ABOUT TO GET QUIET.

WHAT THE HELL IS THIS? YOU HAVE ANY IDEA WHAT THESE GUYS WERE UP TO?

WHO KNOWS WITH THESE NUT JOBS?

"IT'S JUST SOME CRAZY MACHINE. HOW MUCH DAMAGE COULD IT DO?"

CLINK
HERE'S TO A JOB WELL DONE.
LET'S SEE. CITY PLUNGED INTO DARKNESS, LOTS OF PROPERTY DAMAGE, THOUGH FORTUNATELY FEW INJURIES AND NO DEATHS WE DID NOT CAUSE. KHAN ESCAPED.
HOW COULD I HAVE EVER DOUBTED YOU, CRANSTON?
GLASS HALF FULL, DEAR GIRL. KHAN'S BASE OF OPERATIONS HAS BEEN DESTROYED, HIS INCOME STREAM CRUSHED, AND ORGANIZED CRIME IN THIS CITY HAS TAKEN A SERIOUS HIT.
I SUPPOSE WHEN YOU PUT IT THAT WAY, IT DOESN'T SEEM LIKE A TOTAL DISASTER.
PLUS, WE STILL HAVE THESE LOVELY ACCOMMODATIONS.
THAT'S THE SPIRIT. I'LL TELL YOU SOMETHING ELSE. WE'VE MADE OUR MARK. YOU CAN'T DOUBT IT NOW. NO ONE WILL DOUBT IT NOW.
DOUBT WHAT?
THAT THE SHADOW IS BACK.

ISSUE #1 RETAILER SHARED EXCLUSIVE COVER

ART BY ARDIAN SYAF INKS BY GUILLERMO ORTEGA COLORS BY KYLE RITTER

CLASSIC SHADOW TALES! REMASTERED AND BACK IN PRINT!

THE SHADOW: BLOOD & JUDGMENT TPB
978-1-60690-327-8
Howard Chaykin

THE SHADOW MASTER SERIES VOL. 1 TPB
ISBN13: 978-1-60690-482-4
Andrew Helfer, Bill Sienkiewicz

THE SHADOW MASTER SERIES VOL. 2 TPB
ISBN13: 978-1-60690-482-4
Andrew Helfer, Kyle Baker

THE SHADOW 1941: HITLER'S ASTROLOGER HC
978-1-60690-4429-9
Denny O'Neil, Michael W. Kaluta

Visit us online at **www.DYNAMITE.com**
Follow us on Twitter **@dynamitecomics**
Like us on Facebook **/Dynamitecomics**
Watch us on YouTube **/Dynamitecomics**